A CENTURY OF
JAPANESE
MOTORCYCLES

This edition first published in 2001 by MBI Publishing Company,
Galtier Plaza, Suite 200, 380 Jackson St., St. Paul, MN 55101

© E-T-A-I, 2000

Graphic Design : Isabelle Cransac
Translation : Kevin Desmond and Gerald G. Guetat

Previously published by E-T-A-I, 20, rue de la Saussière – 92100 Boulogne-Billancourt, France

MBI Publishing Company books are also available at discounts in bulk quantity for industrial or sales-promotional use.
For details write to Special Sales Manager at Motorbooks International Wholesalers & Distributors,
Galtier Plaza, Suite 200, 380 Jackson St., St. Paul, MN 55101
Library of Congress Cataloging-in-Publication Data Available.

ISBN : 0-7603-1190-0

Printed in Spain

Title : A Century of Japanese Motorcycles
ISBN # 0-7603-1190-0
Retail price : $29.95US

A CENTURY OF
JAPANESE
MOTORCYCLES

Didier Ganneau — François-Marie Dumas

MBI Publishing Company

To Yori Kanda,
whose faithful friendship over more than twenty years
and great culture,
as much European as Japanese, have enabled us to better
interpret the mysteries of this saga.

THANKS

The authors warmly thank all those who have enabled us to complete this work and in particular :
Yori Kanda, our most precious interface between the European and Japanese cultures, who opened the doors
of this country for us ; Kikuo Iwatate, undisputed specialist in the history of the motorcycle in Japan
and in particular of its beginnings ; Mitsuru Nakaoki, who honored us by writing the preface
to this work and has enriched it with numerous illustrations.

Also thanks
To the makers :
Honda, Kawasaki, Suzuki and Yamaha, but also Bridgestone, Daihatsu, Fuji-Subaru, Mazda and Mitsubishi,
their importers and press offices
To enthusiasts who generously made their collections and their archives
available to us, notably Claude Millard (Suzuki), Gérard Lachambre (Aulnay Motos Pièces),
Ludy Beumer (Yamaha Motor Europe), Yves Campion, Pierre Ducloux and Sammy Miller.
To the museums who welcomed us, including the Honda Collection Hall,
the Asama Memorial Cottage, the Asagiri Kogen Museum,
the Nigata Motorcycle Museum and the Tokyo Transport Museum.
The journalists, photographers and historians, who have offered us their advice,
notably Christian Lacombe, Michel Montange and Bertrand Thiebault of Moto-Journal,
Jean-Pierre Boulmé, Carlo Bagalini, Cyril Barthe, Marc Francotte, Christian Bedeï,
Pierre Leguévaques, Denis Meunier, Stan Perec and Mick Woollett.
To the secretary of the JAMA (Japan Automobile Manufacturers Association)
who provided us with numerous statistics of sales and of production.

Contents

富士山の近くにある私の仕事場に、デュマさん夫妻とディディエさん、そして私の友人の神田穎樹さんが来てくれたのは2年前のことでした。

そのとき、挨拶のあとですぐに私に向けられた、「モーターサイクルのサンヨーとエレクトロニクスのサンヨーは関係があるのか?」という最初の質問で、私はデュマさんとディディエさんの日本のモーターサイクルに対する知識の深さに大きな尊敬の念を抱きました。

フランスは自転車を生み、育てあげた国であり、モーターサイクルのパイオニア期にもドイオンをはじめ、多くのモーターサイクルを誕生させて世界中に影響を及ぼしました。

日本でもプジョーの自転車は早くから知られていましたし、1920年代には冒険心に満ちた富裕な人たちがモーターサイクルを楽しみはじめました、プジョー、モトベカーヌ、テロー、ルネジレーといったモーターサイクルの名前は、そのころから知られていましたし、飛行桜が大好きだった私は子供のころに、ノームローヌという名前に憧れていました。

多くのことをフランスをはじめとするヨーロッパの国々から学んで作りはじめられた日本のモーターサイクルは、不幸な戦争によって、その成長が中断されました。1945年、つまり戦争に敗れた年の生産台数は127台で、それも敗戦の8月までに作られた軍用の陸王がほとんどで、アサヒ、メグロといったモーターサイクルは数台しか作られませんでした。

占領軍は1946年に月産1500台のトラック製造を許可しましたが、あらゆる資材の不足によって生産はその1/3程度にしかなりませんでした。ただし、モーターサイクルの生産に対しては制限がなかったために、1946年には、残存した軍用小型発電機用の小さなエンジンを自転車に取り付けたものが走りはじめ、在庫がなくなると町の小さなエンジンを作り、ビスモーターやホンダといった、"自転車バイク"が重い荷を積んで伝まはじめました。

少悪なガソリンとオイル、そして積み過ぎといった過酷な条件のなかから

M. Nakaoki (left) interviewing a veteran Meguro rider during a reunion at the Asama Meeting Club.

自転車バイクのエンジンは90ccから125ccに成長し、たとう10台しか作らなかったとしても、名前を残した工場の数は200社をこえ、1952年の総生産台数は50ccを含めて9万台に達しましたが、耐久性はそしく、そのために外国車の上陸が急増しました。

日本の役所は国産車を育てるために輸入関税を高くしながら、一部のメーカーに助成金を支出しました、役所の主導による耐久長距離テストも行われたが、民間主導で1953年に行われた"名古屋TT"のほうが、はるかに有効でした。このレースの直後にホンダは、「国内市場の事い合いは貴重な資源を浪費するだけであり、これからは輸出によって国家経済の再建に貢献するべきだ」という声明を発表しましたが、当時この声明は正当に評価されることはありませんでした。

名古屋TTの出場車が150ccに限定されたあと、国産車は250cc全盛の時代に入りますが、スポーツモデルが本格的に登場したのは1960年からで。

それらは1955年から1959年に行われた"浅間火山レース"の経験を生かして作られました。マン島TTに初めて出場したホンダの125cc、ワークス・マシンも"浅間育ち"でした。

いっ、どの車からジャパンオリジナルなのか、という質問に私は、C70と答えることにしています。C70は1959年のマン島のあと、まずオランダに輸出されて好評を得てからヨーロッパの各国に送られたからです。

C70系とYDSの成功で幕をあけた1960年代は、日本のモーターサイクルたちが最もエネルギッシュに、最も光り輝やいた時代でした。それは、それぞれが個性的だったからですが、良い物を作っても開発スピードが遅かったり、マネージメントが伴わないメーカーは1960年代に次々に脱落していきました。ライラックの丸正に代表される悲劇を思うと、1960年代は最もエキサイティングだった反面で、最もつらく悲しい時代だったのでした。

考えてみると1950年代はじめころの日本のバイクたちは一般大衆の生きるための足として、酷使に耐えて伝み続け、そこには、そのあと現在に至る日本のモーターサイクルの隆盛と華やかさを予知できるものはありませんでした。敗戦後の貧困のなかで生まれたバイクから、現在のモーターサイクルまで、それを正確に記述することは、本来、日本人がするべきこと、と私は考えていますが、たいへん残念なことに、この国ではそのように厖大な仕事量を積み重ねた本は1社から出版されただけであるのに対して、このたびフランスでこのように立派な本が出版されることについて、ひとりの日本人として美望を感じながら、日本のモーターサイクルの歴史…それも自国のモーターサイクルの歴史を、ひとつの文化としてとらえて懐ろの深さに、心からの敬意と感謝を捧げたいと思っています。

そしてデュマさんとディディエさん、関係の皆さんにも心から「ありがとう」と申しあげます。

年6月

中沖 満

Foreword

BY MITSURU NAKAOKI

PRESIDENT OF THE ASAMA MEETING CLUB •HISTORIAN-RESTORER- ILLUSTRATOR

Two years ago, I had a visit from my friend, Yori Kanda, accompanied by two French journalists. Soon after the introductions, came the first question : is there a connection between the motorbike make Sanyo and the electronics firm today known under this name ? The stage was set : those guys already knew more about the Japanese motorbike than even our specialists.

France was the cradle of the bicycle, and can count itself among motorbike pioneers, even if only thanks to the Marquis de Dion. Peugeot bikes were known in Japan from the beginning of the century, and makes like Terrot, Motobécane or René Gillet were very much appreciated there during the 1920s. Personally, when I was a kid, as an airplane enthusiast, I had a soft spot for the Gnome-Rhône. And it was through inspiration from French and European motorbikes that the Japanese industry took off.

In 1946, the Americans authorized the revival of the two-wheel industry, and one could start building little machines, equipped with engines from electric generators. Because of the mediocre quality of fuels and lubricants, but also because of the chronic excess weight of these vehicles, it quickly became necessary to increase the capacity of these small engines. And every bit as rapidly, one witnessed a frenetic rivalry between close to two hundred builders.

Despite everything, the quality of their products left much to be desired. The Japanese authorities, to improve local production, introduced tough importation taxes and financially participated in the growth of the most dynamic builders.

They would also support the organization of endurance races but it was with the Nagoya TT in 1953, organized in a totally private manner, that things really took off.

Soon after this event, S. Honda announced : "Competition for the home market is only a waste of time and energy. From now on, we must place the accent on export to contribute to the rebuilding of our economy." At that time, nobody really took any notice of this little speech.

The machines competing on the Nagoya TT had been limited to 150 cc. Afterwards, it was the 250 Class which became more popular, and true sportsmen made their appearance from the start of the 1960s. They had held their own in races around Mount Asama between 1955 and 1959. Even the first Honda 125s taking part in the Isle of Man TT had grown up on the slopes of this volcano.

To the question : "What would be the first real Japanese motorbike ?", I would reply the Honda C70. It was exported to the Netherlands just after the 1959 TT and immediately gained an excellent reputation. It was the first to make a real impact in Europe. Its success, that of its heirs and that of the Yamaha YDS in the 1960s turned this decade into the most glorious and the most dynamic ever known by the Japanese motorbike.

Each make had its own personality and character, but the time of the "Big Four" had come. All the models were of good quality, but either arriving too late or suffering from poor business organization, the other makes disappeared one by one. In the image of Marusho-Lilac, the 1960s were without doubt the most exciting, but also the most dramatic in the history of the Japanese motorbike.

When one looks at what happened during the 1950s, the Japanese motorbike was being used above all as a means of transport, vital for the average citizen. It was absolutely necessary for it to be reliable, and one could never have imagined the formidable escalation which was going to liven up this industry so soon after.

To describe this evolution from its post-war poverty right up until the present opulence, could only, I thought, be done by a Japanese. However, the unique work in which I have discovered the complete chronology of all these events is the one you are about to read. It has, I know, demanded much time and work, and I am full of admiration. I have the greatest respect for this formidable body of research, and I congratulate the authors for having known how to deal with the cultural side of the Japanese motorbike.

To François-Marie, to Dider, and to all those who have made publication of this book possible, a warm "arigato" (thank-you), from the bottom of my heart.

—*Mitsuru Nakaoki*

The virtual motorbike

Insular, Japan developed in almost total autarky until the nineteenth century. It was certainly influenced by China from the first to the ninth century, but thereafter it developed its own culture, its own writing, its own religion. It was, therefore, protected from any external interference, under the authority of a tough feudal system. According to certain revisionists, Marco Polo never set foot in Japan in the eighteenth Century.

（石油発動自轉車）

1896（明29）年1月21日付毎日新聞「石油発動自転車試運転

Here, just over a century ago is the first motorbike imported into Japan, a Hildebrand Wolfmüller shipped out from Germany. Tokyo, January 19th, 1896. (Doc. Kikuo Iwatate)

t was not until 1853 that the American Commander Perry entered into "normal" relations with this country emerging from the Middle Ages. Clearly, he compelled Japan to enter into unfavorable commercial exchanges. Might one find in this unbalanced agreement, the reasons for the very protectionism for which one would soon be reproaching Japan? Anyway, since 1868 the Meiji era marked a definite opening up to the West… but already one-way. Without losing anything of its personality, Japan integrated Western lifestyles, digesting them so as to pull out the best aspects while still protecting itself. In 1911, she elaborated her own Customs system. Until then, Japan had been forbidden to fix her own customs laws.

The motorbike, very early on

It was in this period of openness to Western techniques and ideas that the first imported motorcycle rolled over the Japanese soil in 1896.

In January, Shinsuke Jumonji, member of the House of Representatives, gave demonstrations with a Hildebrand Wolfmüller in front of the Hibiya Hotel. This German machine, being, since 1894, nothing less than the first motorbike in the world to be mass-produced, one can but imagine the sensational curiosity that this original created right in the heart of Tokyo! Following this, some de Dion engines and Gladiator tricycles were seen in Japan, but it was above all American motorbikes : Thomas tricycles followed by Mitchell then Indian motorbikes, which were the first to be imported at the beginning of the century.

N. Shimazu invents the Japanese motorbike

In 1902, Shintaro Yoshida, owner of a cycle store, built the first Japanese automobile with help from his young employee Komanosuke Uchiyama. It was powered by an American engine. In 1907, the total number of Japanese cars stood at sixteen, and Uchiyama produced the Takuri, first car with a home-built gas engine. On two wheels, the first Japanese motorbikes carried different names but they were almost all the work of the same man, N. Shimazu, to whom we also owe more than two hundred patents related to engines. Helped by Torao Yamaba, another motor vehicle pioneer in Japan (he built a steam-powered bus in 1904), Shimazu built his first engine in 1908. The following year, he fitted it into a bicycle frame,

This drawing of a Panhard and Levassor, from the pen of Georges Ferdinand Bigot, immortalizes the first automobile run around Tokyo, on February 19th, 1898, between Tsukiji and Ueono. The magazine "La France Automobile" of April 16th would report on the event. The engineer, Jean-Marie Thevenet, here at the wheel, met with no success when he tried to import such horseless carriages.

creating what is accepted as the first entirely Japanese motorbike. Called the NS, this bulky unsprung bike was powered by a 397 cc single-cylinder unit with automatic inlet valve (76 x 87.5 mm). Shimazu had also made the carburetor.

Four years later, Shimazu designed the NMC (Nippon Motor Manufacturing), a 250 cc clearly inspired by Triumphs, of which the only non-Japanese component was the German origin magneto. They sold around twenty of these at the fabulous price of two hundred to two hundred and fifty yen. A colossal figure when one realizes that at the time a Tokyo policeman was being paid a monthly salary of eight yen and fifty cents!

One rediscovers NMC and the realization of the same Shimazu under a new label as of 1925 : Aero Fast. The first model, a 633 cc single cylinder with side valves, was hardly distributed. It was noted for its gearbox, which included a reverse gear for side-car use. Two years later a new Aero Fast was introduced, this time a 250 cc with a two-speed gearbox, which met with great success with some seven hundred units sold.

Meanwhile, in 1913, one of the first great makes had appeared in the form of Asahi, set up by a man named Miyata, already well known for his arms and bicycles. With the exception of the fuel-tank decoration, one might have sworn that this was a 550 cc Triumph and this was not by chance. Mr. Maeda, of Nagoya, had had a Triumph delivered to Mr. Miyata, who had had a replica made of it by a certain Negishi. Priced at four

The very primitive N.S. of 1909, photographed in Osaka where it was built, was probably the first true Japanese motorbike. (Document Kikuo Iwatate)

selling a good thousand machines to Japan each year. Other countries good at exporting, Belgium (Sarolea, Gillet, F.N.) and especially Great Britain (AJS, BSA, Matchless, Norton, Triumph) were also well represented. Nor was it long before Husqvarna and Moto-Guzzi had established themselves, followed by BMW in 1927.

1923 : an earthquake that acted as detonator

On September 1st, 1923, Tokyo was shaken by the largest earthquake in modern times. The quake caused more than twenty thousand deaths and showed up an outmoded transport network, a vulnerability of rail routes and a crying lack of rescue vehicles.
Reconstruction would make of Tokyo a city slightly more open to circulation and its needs for motorized vehicles would be met by a variety of importers, then of makers. The sum total of vehicles increased from 12,700 units in 1923 to 24,300 in 1924.
In 1924 two important motorbike firms were born—Rikuo and Murato. The second would commercialize using Giant engines designed by K Uchiyama, already mentioned.
These national initiatives were supported the following year by the institution of an import surcharge, which at the same time would favour the setting-up of local businesses exploiting American technology, as least with the automobile.
Ford installed a factory at Yokohama in 1924, General Motors followed in Osaka in 1927, and Chrysler in 1929.

hundred and eighty yen, this first Asahi was used by the Tokyo police and served as escort for the Prime Minister. Miyata and his Asahi provisionally closed down in 1916, but the firm would be reborn under these two names (or under that of Miyapet for mopeds) and was slogging on until 1964. They are still making bicycles today.

The milieu takes shape

The first highway code was published in 1919. As with the laws of the period, it was inspired by the British system, then very influential since Japan and Great Britain had been allies since 1902. So it was decided to drive on the left-hand side, but to remain realistic : Japan was not ripe for popular motoring. The road network was virtually non-existent, and the towns inextricably grew up with this. Those using motor vehicles were above all the military.
The war against Russia in 1944 and the annexing of Korea in 1910 highlighted the importance of transport systems for both troops and equipment. And in 1918, a law enabled the army to subsidize civilian makers, provided they produced requisition vehicles in time of war. At the start of the 1920s, Japan was already counted among the big world economic powers,

particularly thanks to its strong textile industry : since 1915, the export/import balance was positive, and a Ministry of Commerce was created in 1925.
The motorcycle industry was still embryonic but imports were going in the right direction. Most of them arrived from the United States, relatively nearby : around 1925, Harley-Davidson and Indian were each

Intricate street maps in Japanese cities

The anarchic plan of Japanese towns is a heritage of permanent conflicts between cities that had been laying waste to Japan until the nineteenth century. It was therefore necessary to design deliberately complicated town plans to prevent enemy penetration. With neither horses nor cars, travel was by foot. Even today, Tokyo, without the skills of a Baron Haussmann after the 1923 earthquake, the roads rarely carry names and the numbering of the buildings resides in a complex system based on blocks.
All of a sudden, and even more than two- and four-wheel vehicles, it was tricycles and side-cars which took advantage following the earthquake. And for a purely practical reason : in the maze of Japanese cities, only very easy-to- handle, narrow and relatively light machines were capable of weaving in and out. Anyone who has ever adventured in the streets of Naples will understand that such machines were enjoying their moment of glory in Italy during the same period.
And yet, in this context, the usefulness of a motorbike was reserved for simply running around. The three-wheeler was ideal for transporting goods. Around 1930, there were over four thousand side-cars and tricycles compared with around ten thousand motorbikes registered in Japan.

Opposite : No, this is not a Triumph but a period shot of its replica, the Asahi, built by Miyata in 1913. Note that the rider has kept his traditional wooden-soled geta while a retouched bush hides a motorbike stand if not also an incomplete transmission. (Document Kikuo Iwatate)

Neither the Japanese-style topography nor the signposts in the same language appeared to simplify life for Frenchman Henri Andrieux. Together with Robert Sexé, who took this photo, Andrieux crossed Japan during a 1926 world tour at the handlebars of their Belgium Gillet motorcycles. Here they are north of Kyoto.

During their voyage to Japan in 1926, the motorcycles of Robert Sexé and Henri Andrieux make a stop in front a bicycle shop.

Belgium was the one of the most represented European countries in Japan during the 1920s and this photo was taken in 1924 for the catalogue of Kotobuki-Ya, importer for Saroléa based in Osaka.

Tesuji Makita, one of the most famous pioneer engineers of the motorbike in Japan, created the Japan Automobile Company (JAC/Nippon Jidosha 1928-1934). Here is his first model (right), photographed in 1929 in front of the factory at Shinagawa (Tokyo). JAC would make motorbikes under its own name then engines that would power other labels of the same group: Aikoku ("who loves one's country" 1933-1938), and Kurogane (1937-1959). From the former make came 350 and 500 cc side-valve models around 1933 and a V-twin 500 looking like the JAP, while in 1931 Nippon Jidosha (who had in 1928 built one of the first Japanese tricycles) produced about thirty examples of an astonishing 1,200 cc flat-twin destined for the Imperial escort (below).

A club reunion in the early 1920s

Kenzo Tada, national hero

Racing during this period was active enough, even though events more often consisted of coastal racing, systematically contested on unmade tracks.

The leading rider of the period was Kenzo Tada. After having brilliantly begun his career in bicycle-racing, he went over to the motorbike at thirty-four years old, in 1921, winning the first race he entered. When in 1930 he decided to take part in the Tourist Trophy on the Isle of Man, it was an entire expedition : eight hours by boat as far as Korea, ten days by train as far as Warsaw, crossing Germany and Belgium. He needed two weeks to reach the temple of motorcycle racing.

Classed twenty-eighth in the trials out of forty-two entries, at the handlebars of his 350 Velocette KTT he managed to finish fifteenth for the seven laps which made up the race. It was an real exploit, which gained him a bronze medal.

The legend continued. Returning to his country, fêted as a hero, he attributed his performance to his Lodge 341 PP spark plug whose insulating material had been made with a black mica, then unknown in Japan. He therefore invested his entire fortune in a mica deposit, buying up nothing less than a mountain to the north of Korea ! Not only did the war put an end to his mining activities, but it ended up by ruining him when Japan had to pull out of Korea.

Kenzo Tada returned to competition in 1948, cycling first then motorbiking. He would also be at the origins of the foundation of MFJ in 1951 (Motorcycle Federation of Japan) becoming consultant for DSK then Suzuki, coming back to take part in a few Grand Prix (such as the TT). He never stopped encouraging motorcycle racing in Japan.

In the 1920s, imports got going, even for the famous American Briggs and Stratton Motor-Wheel.

1931 : a conflict as catalyst

Like the rest of the world, in 1929 Japan felt the repercussions of the economic crisis. By the autumn, the yen had lost half the value it had held against the dollar in 1924. A new military government came to power in 1931. It had protectionism as its credo, and intended to boost national industry through military orders that would serve its expansionist policy in Manchuria. Soon Europe would come to know the same warlike and xenophobic temptations. In May

1931, a committee for the establishment of a domestic automobile industry was created and the latest regulations were not slow in favoring tricycles. Their dimensions could be increased, their performance was stepped up (25 mph instead of 15 mph), their transport payload went up to 413 lbs. Such factors would make them kings of Japanese traffic with the army, alongside small four-wheeled commercial vehicles,

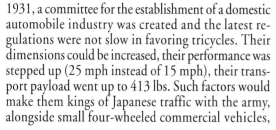

March 1926. Photo call for the three winners of the Shizuoka Championship. From left to right : K. Nose (2 1/2 hp BSA Super Sports), Matsumoto (2 1/2 hp single-cylinder Harley-Davidson) and Kawabata (2 3/4 hp New Imperial).

The young Miyata, rider of a real "Made in England" Triumph entered by the Kansai Autobi Club of Osaka. He has just won the Japanese TT, an endurance race of 470 miles, run in 1925 between Osaka and Tokyo.

also much prized by the military. One of the first tricycles, the New Era, was built by Nippon Jidosha of Tokyo in 1928. Nine years later, the same vehicle, under the Kurogane label, was being made at five factories specializing in the three-wheelers and military equipment.

Between 1930 and 1936, when production of two wheelers was stagnating at around fifteen hundred units, tricycles were taking off, production going from three hundred units in 1930 to fifteen thousand two hundred and thirty in 1937. The two major actors in this boom were Tokyo Kogyo (Mazda) and Daihatsu. Motorcycle production standards at the beginning of

Race start in 1926. From front to back: two Saroleas, a Norton, a Triumph and a Douglas.

Etablished right in the heart of Tokyo, Yamada Rinseikwan (literally "the wheels of success of Yamada") was the largest importer of the period and distributed the biggest makes. We see here, in 1926, in front of their shop window and from left to right: a four-cylinder Ace, an Indian Scout, an Excelsior and a Harley-Davidson. A quarter of a century later, M. Yamada, would become manufacturer of the Yamarin, and then Hosk, labels.

This pretty-faced starlets of the Japanese cinema in the middle of the 1920s, poses for publicity photos at the handlebars of a Saroléa, as is written on the fuel tank and the front plate.

Very representative of the pre-war Japanese market, this Lion tricycle manufactured in Osaka in about 1930 was powered by an English JAP engine made in London. Lack of supplies caused Lion's bankruptcy in 1933.

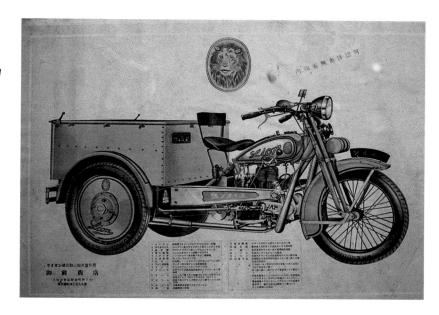

Before the Sino-Japanese conflict of 1937, imports from Europe or the United States still made up the majority of the fleet. Here side-by-side in 1935 are an Indian and a BSA Sloper. For those used to writing in pictograms, notice the order of the characters was not primordial : the front plate of the "BSA" was acronymed "ASB".

Daihatsu : above all commercial

The roots of Daihatsu go back to 1907, the year the firm developed an engine running on natural gas. Their first tricycle, in December 1930, was without doubt the first of its type in Japan and it would be quickly appreciated. The tricycle tradition would remain strong at Daihatsu over the years, since the Midget of 1957 would be produced until late in the 1960s, even though the firm was already very involved with car-making. One must say that their first four-wheeler did not appear until 1963 : their previous automobiles had only been coachbuilt tricycles.

This first Daihatsu HA tricycle of 1930, with its 500 cc side-valve engine was the pioneer of a long tradition. The firm devoted itself for a long time to tricycles, in particular with the Midget which appeared in 1957. The first Daihatsu four-wheelers only appeared in 1963.

Like Daihatsu (which would ultimately take them over), Tsubasa was established in Osaka and began to build tricycles from 1931 with a side-valve 500. Their 1934 range included the 6.5 and 7.5 hp, powered by side-valve V-twins imported from Great Britain. Notice the stamped sheet metal frame and the curious suspension in front of the power wheel.

Mazda : the waverer

Hiroshima was very early in its interest in motoring and Toyo Kogyo (better known today under the name of Mazda) became involved with the motorbike in 1930. However, from 1931, the firm only devoted itself to the tricycle. They were making up to five hundred per month in 1949, and remained faithful to this type of light vehicle until 1960, the definitive date for their transferring to four-wheel manufacture.

During the 1930s, Mazda produced an entire range of tricycles, 500 cc or 650 cc, side-valve single cylinders, with payloads ranging from two hundred to five hundred kilos. The three-point Mitsubishi star also appeared on the fuel tank because this huge consortium supplied engines for these tricycles.

The unique Mazda motorbike, of which only about thirty were produced.

the 1930s, as shown by Aero Fast (Shimazu-engined), SSD end Ritsurin (350 and 500 four-stroke single-cylinders) or Myiata (175 cc two-stroke) was still very traditional and inspired as much by Great Britain as by the United States. Besides, the majority of the motorbikes sold were based on imported elements. However, importing became harder and harder as Japan became increasingly belligerent. In 1935, the military authorities favored a certain number of firms with important markets while the other manufacturers, deprived of any materials, had no other option than to stop their activities. The army had very precisely defined the contract conditions, Types 97, 98, 99 and 00. The biggest orders concerned Type 97 based on the 1,200 cc Rikuo (alias Harley), introduced in 1935. This machine would therefore be legally copied by the factories of Kurogane, Aikoku, Toko Kogyo, and SSD. A great story besides, is that of SSD, created in the middle of the 1920s by the Shishido brothers in Hiroshima. They were far from the industrial center so, through lack of local subcontractors, SSD started off by making a copy of the Triumph 350, building everything themselves (including the spokes and the bearings). Only the Bosch magneto was imported. Miraculously, in 1931, SSD obtained a subsidy of one hundred million yen (a million dollars) and developed a 1,200 cc V-twin. There were even a few prototypes where the rear-wheel was replaced by a swinging trolley supporting two small double wheels. It was designed at the request of the Japanese army to support its invasion of China, where a lack of bridges required crossing fords.

The twin-cylinder Vs copied on the Rikuo model would be produced from 1937 to 1945 in the JAC factories, using successively the JAC, Aikoku, then Kurogane labels as 1,260 then 750 cc models. The 1,260 cc Kurogane of 1939 was from the outset designed with a machine-gun support. After the hostilities, Kurogane would come under the control of another of Japan's great engineers, Otha Tokyu, and would become Nippon Nainenki then Tokyu Kurogane. It would close its doors in 1959.

1937 : state of war

In 1936, a law imposed government approval on any builder planning to annually produce more than three thousand vehicles of over 750 cc. At the same time, a top annual limit of 12,360 vehicles was established.

The Americans did not particularly appreciate this poor joke, which rendered all their on-site investments null and void. But young national manufacturers, on the other hand, showed no hesitation in profiting from this, recuperating the networks and suppliers set up by the Americans. Toyota brought out their first automobile in 1935 and Meguro made a start on the motorbike in 1937. In general, the entire national motorbike industry was boosted by this law... and by import taxes which went from 74 to 560 yen in January 1937 ! At a time when a Harley-Davidson with side-car cost 2,680 yen, or an entirely new 500 Meguro displayed at 950 yen, it was one hell of a price...

Strategic sector

At the same time, the start of the Sino-Japanese conflict in August 1937 marked the taking off of the two-wheeler... and of all the other types of transport. In favor of a planned economy, the state had been helping out the industry. The motorbike, as well as the car and aviation were in an ideal position. These sectors were considered strategic as much by the autonomy of movement that they provided, by the diversity of technologies that they called for. Whoever controlled vehicle construction, from rubber production right up to electrical fittings, upholstery and glazing, while passing through all the stages of metal-working, was really in a position to dominate the world. Suddenly, two-wheel manufacture, which was running at around a thousand to fifteen hundred units per year between 1930 and 1936, was increased to between two thousand and three thousand units from 1937 and 1943. Production of tricycles fell back rapidly after 1937, while that of four-wheelers (essentially commercial) took off to reach 45,682 vehicles in 1941. The Japanese motorbike was still for the future. The automobile industry act and the five-year plan linked to it in 1937 were ambitious, and the War Ministry clearly classified the automobile (logically taking in the motorbike) among the key military industries for controlled shareholders and management. From 1938, priority was given to "commercial" production, to the detriment of civilian production and builders unambiguously came under government control.

Fatal spiral

In March 1938, the Act of General Mobilisation further increased the dependency of the makers on controlling prices, salaries, investments and credit. The electrical industry was nationalized and the distribution of steel closely monitored. In August, civilian production was interrupted in favor of military or community vehicles. In 1939, the first day of each month was declared a free workday for the state and gas was rationed. The pact with Italy and Germany was signed in 1940, and when petroleum imports coming from the USA were stopped in 1941 (before the raid on Pearl Harbor), conversion to the alternative fuels became the priority. This more or less nationalized industrial status would prove a major advantage after the war. The makers would have established close almost exclusive relationships of confidence and mutual solidarity with their suppliers during the ordeal. And this network of satellites would remain precious in times of peace.

Rikuo : America taken hostage

Created by Alfred R. Child, the first Harley-Davidson agency was set up in Japan in 1923 and these machines were soon equipping the police, the army, and even the Imperial escort. Distribution was ensured by Rikuo ("King of the road"). Following the devaluation of the yen in 1929, it became more profitable to assemble the Harleys in Japan and to build them under license. At the end of 1932, when a 1,200 Harley-Davidson cost 1,890 yen and the salary of a banking employee stood at 90 yen per month, Harley-Davidson reached an industrial agreement with Rikuo. A 750 cc. assembled in Japan appeared in 1934 followed, in 1935, by a 1,200 cc entirely made in Japan. Harley did not make much profit out of this. A Japan which was becoming militarized did not hesitate in granting the licence to other factories. Child was sent back to the United States in 1937 and Rikuo continued manufacture on its own, with American tooling, without paying any rights at all to Harley-Davidson ! Feeble consolation : Ford, GM, and Chrysler suffered the same fate and themselves had to abandon all their personnel on site before 1939, without the slightest compensation. This is without doubt the episode which gave Japan, and for a long time, a heavy reputation for inelegance in business relationships.

So up to 1942, in the southern suburb of Tokyo, Rikuo produced eighteen thousand 1,200 cc machines, strictly identical to the Harley-Davidson VLs, then devoted themselves to the production of torpedoes until the end of hostilities. Rikuo were not entirely satisfied with simple copies and, in 1936, the engineer M. Sakurai created the first Japanese coupling to a side-car on the base of the 1200 cc. The chain-drive on the rear wheel of the motorbike was kept, while a shaft drove the side-car wheel. After the war, Rikuo resumed production of models strictly derived from Harleys, with a 750 cc from 1947, then a 1200 cc starting in 1950. These were the most powerful bikes then produced in Japan. The range was completed in 1953 by a 350 cc shaft-drive single-cylinder model, much inspired by BMW technology, overtaken in 1958 by a 250 cc version. But everything has an end. Japan, in going off to seduce the United States, simultaneously re-opened its doors to Harley-Davidson, resulting in the definitive closing of Rikuo in 1962.

Harley-Davidson publicity in Japan in 1933. Four years later, the motorbike had scarcely changed but it would only carry the Rikuo label.

The Rikuo 750 cc of 1953 was close to the famous Harley WL 45s, and just as rustic : side-valve and no rear suspension but, as compensation, luxurious big tires of 5.00 x 16 inches.

The 1200 cc Rikuo (1935) was no different from the Harley-Davidson except for its acronym. The large, side-valve single-cylinder was coupled to a four-speed gearbox and pushed out 28 hp, 60 mph for 1,267 lbs. with its side-car. Rikuo would also develop a version with powered side-car wheel in production between 1938 and 1939.

This ultimate prototype Rikuo 750 RX with rocker valves, conceived in 1960, would have to follow on from the rustic RTI. More original than previous versions, it resembled all the best in Harley technology in a single model (Asama Memorial Cottage document).

The reconstruction

The war caused over two million deaths. It also repatriated three million colonists from occupied or annexed territories (such as Taiwan since 1895). It is estimated that 40 percent of the towns were razed to the ground ; the bombing of Tokyo alone in March 1945 involved one hundred thousand deaths, almost as many victims as Hiroshima or Nagasaki.

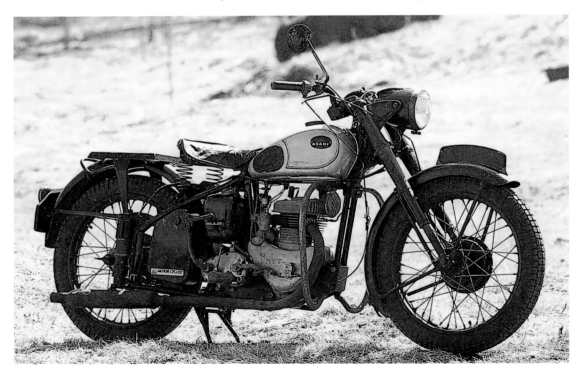

In 1954, this side-valve Asahi 250 FA2 Golden Beam had just as much British influence as the previous models.
Its 7.6 hp took its 322 lbs. to 54 mph. (Asama Memorial Cottage document)

conomically shattered, Japan was under American political supervision. The headquarters of the Allied Forces authorized the revival of a road vehicle industry from the outset, but priority was obviously given to goods transport. In 1945, 686 tricycles and 6,892 commercial four-wheelers were produced and practically no private vehicles. At any rate, inflation was such that retail prices would triple in 1946, and, the average Japanese had other concerns besides the automobile or the motorbike.

At first, the restriction on automobile production favored the comeback of the two-wheeler all the same. Asahi was the first post-war builder to return to regular production, with its 200 cc DC, directly developed from its 175 cc AA of 1935. And in 1946, two major makes appeared : Pointer and Showa. They would make their mark.

Three vitamins for an economy

Three factors would boost Japan's re-emergence.

Firstly, the state had been indebted to industry during the war. It at first intended to reimburse the companies directly, but the inflation which followed lead the Americans to forbid this indemnification in February 1946. In exchange, from then on the government and the Bank of Japan would loan capital at preferential rates. Thus was born the typically Japanese formula of an industry both free-market and at the same time under state supervision, with under-capitalized businesses taking unprecedented risks, guaranteed by the government via the banks. In short, a state-controlled, but not nationalized, economy.

This principle, according to which the Finance Ministry (and not the central bank) fixed interest rates, and according to which the government itself sped up or slowed down this or that sector of the economy, would go on until around 1970. The tradition would continue. Although even recently businesses remained irresponsible for the commercial gambles which they were taking on behalf of shareholders without real power, they were practically assured of state subsidy.

Next, while the military budget represented 44 % of the national budget in 1934, the Constitution laid down by the Americans in 1947 forbade Japan (like Germany) to rearm, placing it under the American military "umbrella". This measure would be progressively

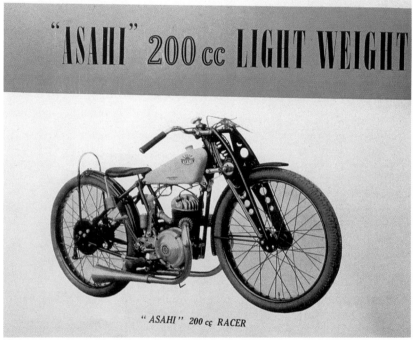

"ASAHI" 200 cc LIGHT WEIGHT

" ASAHI " 200 cc RACER

A make of the Miyata Group, Asahi ("Dawn") made a comeback in 1945, but without renouncing its first loves : the engineering of its DC "Light Weight" seems to come straight from Villiers. The 1950 brochure shows the 200 cc DC in tourist (3 hp) and racing (5.1 hp) versions.

softened afterwards, but the army budget never went above 1 % of the gross national product. At the start of the 1990s, each Japanese was paying no more than two hundred dollars for the defense of his country as opposed to one thousand two hundred dollars from each American. For half a century, in any case, Japan has never poured a quarter of its budget into the army as many western countries have been able to do. The Japanese "self-defense" force has neither bombers nor aircraft carriers, and remains strictly subordinate to the US Army.

Such an "account purification" has enabled Japan to invest colossal budgets not into education, social welfare, or healthcare (sectors which remain fragile) but into the productive economy.

Above all, it has lead an elite of technicians into directing themselves towards the only state-of-the-art industry considered as legal in the absence of aeronautics and military activities, that of land transport. Without doubt, the direct application of the country's entire research's resources has been made, firstly on the fundamental plan and then for robotics and electronics.

Finally, with the Cold War that began in 1947, the Americans judged it necessary to re-establish a real power opposite the Russian and then the Chinese coasts. Their occupation of Japan became less severe and they

In the 1950s, Japan entrusted the transportation of its mail to fleets of Silver Pigeon C-25.

Alongside the Silver Pigeon scooter, Mitsubishi would from 1946 to 1963 be producing an entire line of commercial tricycles under the name of Mizushima. The technology, at first very "motorbike", would evolve towards a form closer to the automobile when Mitsubishi really entered into four-wheels in 1960. This TM3D of 1948 could carry five passengers, as well as the two front open air occupants.

restored a certain autonomy. Car manufacture, at three hundred units per year, was again authorized (it would be entirely liberated in 1949) and a five-year plan was formed in August 1948, which projected the production of one hundred and twenty thousand cars by 1953.

Rabbits, pigeons and a little genius

That said, if "civilian" production finally took off, the average Japanese still went by bicycle ; not astonishing, even in France, motorbikes and fuel would only be freely available in 1949…

Alongside a scatterbrain named of Soichiro Honda, two scooter builders busied themselves in putting Japan back on two wheels.

They were called Fuji and Mitsubishi, and each one introduced a scooter with the respective names of Rabbit (the rabbit is a lucky charm in Japan) and Silver Pigeon (referring to the dove of peace). Both men emerged from aeronautics : the former distinguished himself with his B5N Kate at Pearl Harbor ; the latter became famous in his A6M "Zero". Given such past histories, they no longer had the right to practice their skills in the air, and their redeployment took place.

To launch their very first Rabbit S-1, Fuji did not hesitate to call on female charm.

The first Rabbit S-1 appeared in August 1946 (it had been marketed by November), and the first Silver Pigeon C-10 followed in 1947.
These were only very rudimentary scooters, but the Japanese would give them a phenomenal welcome.

These two manufacturers shared the Japanese market domination right into the middle of the 1950s and only disappeared later into the 1960s.
In little more than twenty years, Fuji and Mitsubishi together produced more than one million scooters.

Honda, the maverick

In 1946 Soichiro Honda was forty years old and had a sound technical training ; he had learned mechanics on the job, in a workshop, then started his own business. He had just sold Toyota his piston-ring factory and found himself with very pretty pile of money. That year he started up the assembly of mopeds, by bolting recuperated army surplus engines onto bicycles. His success was due less to his technological merits than to the fact that with these machines he delivered a fuel he had made up by distilling the resin from local pine trees ! A precious bonus in times of rationing.
His model A, introduced in March 1947, consisted of a home-made engine, still mounted into a

bicycle frame. By October 1948 this model had won over two-thirds of the market sector, at the same time as Honda officially founded the Honda Motor Co. At full capacity Honda would be making one thousand motorbikes per month. Just like Akio Morita, who at the same time was founding the Sony company, Honda was a clever man. But he was also a daredevil who, without the influence of his associates from the outset, K. Kawashima and above all T. Fujisawa, would doubtless have led his enterprise into bankruptcy. To expand, Honda never hesitated to forge ahead and it required all the talents of his two henchmen to channel his energy into less suicidal paths.

The Honda type A was simply an ordinary and modest engine. Destined to be grafted onto bicycles, this little 50 cc two-stroke, with crankcase ignition, belt-drove the rear wheel. Its principle merit was to have arrived at the right moment.

1949-1950 : Sudden halt

The Dodge plan arbitrarily decreed in February 1949 that from then on a dollar was worth 360 yen. This rate notoriously undervalued the yen since the two currencies had been at parity before the war. But it seems that this was the only way to stimulate a still unsteady economy. Where it was concerned, the General Headquarter (GHQ) ended up in November 1949 by lifting all control on production and the sale of civilian vehicles, and a law on the promotion of exports and capital mobility was adopted in May 1950.
Wanting to relaunch the machine too quickly, the Americans instead provoked a sharp rise in inflation. This problem offered at least one advantage : enabling Japan, paradoxically, to develop new social relationships.
Aggressive trade unions and a powerful Left had been well established in Japan since the beginning of the century, and the socialists have even fleetingly taken part in the government in 1947. But as of 1948, the Americans tried to limit union freedom. The right to strike was withdrawn from civil servants in 1949, and a severe "red purge" took place in 1950. With inflation, unemployment, bankruptcies, social tension, violent and long lasting strikes, even hunger strikes, the country was not recovering from the war. Suzuki (which was then still only a textile industry) suffered a strike for over almost six months, which was only settled in May 1950. As for Toyota, this went on for two months (from April to June 1950). From April 1949 to June 1950, the firm was to lose two thousand of its eight thousand jobs, and the automobile industry lost, altogether, 23 % of its workforce.

A new social order

To avoid such troubles happening again, "opposition" unions would gradually be replaced by "in-house" unions. Employment for life, automatic promotion based on seniority, but also social peace by negotiation prior to any strike, the idea of a second family/business (which replaced the idea of father-emperor, broken by the defeat), the circles of quality and multiple-speed enterprise structure : such ideas go back to this period. These are not so much historical, cultural, and innate principles, rather the products of less than half a century, dictated by an economic and social crisis without precedent. One can say that, once these frameworks had been adopted and well established, towards 1955, the "Japan Company" would be ready to step off again

The Maruuchi of 1948 and the Petty of 1950 can be considered as the precursors of the auxiliary-engined bicycle.

A war... salutary ?

The Korean War, which broke out in June 1950, would cause one million deaths. But it was, economically speaking, a godsend for Japan. It boosted orders from the American occupant to local industry and the United States offered advantageous loans for the on-site production of their requirements rather than to have it come from across the Pacific.

The government also encouraged this excellent idea of imposing a 40 % import tax starting in 1951. The March 1952, law promoting industrial rationing clearly classified the automobile, steel, work-tools and electrical industries among the sectors to favour, benefiting from tax exemptions and preferential loan rates.

on the right foot. The motorbike, which did not as yet have a real industrial structure, was less affected by this social revolution. But it would still adopt the new principles : the Honda "in-house" union dates from June 1953. Ultimately, the motorbike would be the first to benefit from this crisis, and it had certainly not been stagnating from 1948 to 1950.

Very centered on scooters (Rabbit and Pigeon alone had over half the whole market in 1950-51), the Japanese motorbike would not have come out of the Stone Age if it had not been for the exceptional personality of Soichiro Honda, and immediately through little engines suitable for bicycles. Bridgestone, Suzuki, Meihatsu, Tohatsu all tackled the motorbike in this humble form around 1952-1953. And when one knows that Meihatsu was an offshoot of Kawasaki Aircraft, one realizes that the future Greats were already there : only Yamaha was missing and would soon arrive.

The Honda Dream : Japan's first real post-war motorbike

The Dream D which Honda introduced in August 1949 was a pivotal event, of which only the name ("Dream") revealed the ambition. This machine marks the first break with pre-war design, in its cleaned-up architecture and modern technology. This was the first Japanese machine with telescopic forks, and its 98 cc two-stroke engine, with crankcase intake, chain-drive, and kick-start, was worthy of the European bikes of the period. As for its frame in stamped sheet metal, it represents the entire Japanese school of the 1950s. Its four-stroke development, the Dream E, would be produced in October 1951 at the rate of five hundred and fifty units per month, a record for Japanese motorcycle manufacturing.

For Honda, 1949 was just as important commercially. In October, the recruitment of T Fujisawa, a highly gifted manager, would help the business pass the bad moments of 1950, notably the setting up a national network (an idea still rare at the time), and by the installation of a branch and a factory in Tokyo. Despite its status as the capital, the city did not at this time carry the commercial weight of Osaka, and Honda's gamble was daring… and visionary.

Above all, if an expanding VS. Honda was improvident, the retiring Fujisawa quickly showed himself

In 1949, the Honda company was still every young but was already showing three models in its catalogue. This 98 cc D-Type was the first really new Japanese motorbike of the post-war era. It produced 3.5 hp at 4,500 rpm and 30 mph.

a formidable businessman. By putting pressure on the suppliers, he owered production costs fall spectacularly—but also bankrupted a number of subcontractors and equipment manufacturers. He would absorb some of these (Showa shock absorbers, Kei Hin carburetors) and would even go as far as to have their own tools made in-house to better control production costs—a field in which Honda is still the champion today. With these strategies he triumphed over his thirty rivals in 1951, grown to seventy by 1952… and one hundred and fifty in 1955 !

In May 1951, Honda unveiled his first four-stroke, the Dream 150 cc E-Type. For over twenty years, Honda would only be producing four-strokes, and from 1951 to 1955, the Dream E would be available in a half dozen versions. Here is a 3E of 1953, with three speeds (only two for the 1951 E) and new stylistic elements such as the lateral frame ribs.

The Puppy of 1953 announced the coming and fleeting domination of Tohatsu on the Japanese market.

With the Meihatsu KB3 of 1954, engine (three-speed) and fuel tank came from Kawasaki. Meihatsu made the bike-frame side and handled its assembly.

Without losing a second, Soichiro Honda left that November to set up his machine-tool trade in the United States. He began again in Europe, in 1954 and 1956, and the first exports left for Taiwan in 1952. As if by chance, the pioneers of this maneuver were Honda and Suzuki, two of the youngest and most dynamic manufacturers on the Japanese motorcycle scene. This deal did not have an immediate follow-up, since Honda only seriously embarked on exportation in 1957, but it was proof of a definite long-term vision.

A railway strike in 1952 gave a timely boost to other forms of transport, including maritime and road. In 1953 Japan became the fifth world manufacturer of two-wheelers, behind Great Britain, Germany, Italy, and France.

As the main competitor of Rabbit and Pigeon, the Jet was a big scooter made by a branch of the big Mitsui Group. This J-3 model of 1954, rustic enough, was a side-valve 215 cc (drawing M. Nakaoki).

In 1952, Tokyo taxis still looked like this Akitsu. Its 142 cc engine only gave 2.5 hp and muscular energy must have come in very useful to move its passengers along at 22 mph. Customers were in the main American soldiers from the Occupation Forces (drawing M. Nakaoki).

Honda : still the right choice

The copy was still a good idea in Japan around 1952-1953.

And it was still Honda who made the best choice. The 90 Benly J, which it launched in August 1953, took its influence from the most advanced machines of the moment, the German NSUs, and more precisely the 100 cc Fox born in 1949.

In Japanese production of the period, this model stood out by its modernity ; it was on a par with the best western references. And Honda, who were employing 150 staff in 1952, would already employ 1,337 by 1953, of an average age younger than twenty-one.

To finance this growth and these adventures, during a major crisis, lest we forget, the firm would invest four hundred and fifty million yen (essentially in tooling) although its capital was only sixty million. Honda had certainly taken all the risks, for which it would pay with a fall in its production in 1954 as well as with the start of the influence of the Mitsubishi Bank on the company.

Like the 1949 NSU Fox 100 cc it copied, the Honda Benly was a big commercial success. With its 89 cc (48 x 49 mm), it developed 3.8 hp at 6,000 rpm, offered only a two-speed gearbox reaching 40 mph. It innovated, in return, with an engine-transmission system that oscillated in rubber blocks working in torsion. This machine certainly heralded the future.

Explosion of the local market

In 1953, the end of the Korean War caused a massive swing back to the motorbike
for numerous industrialists like Suzuki or Yamaha. Production took off and the general craze
for all new types of transport was immense. The first Tokyo Motor Show, from the 20th to 29th of April 1954,
drew five hundred and fifty thousand visitors and two hundred and fifty-four exhibitors.

*As much English as Japanese, the rocker-valve Abe Star FR 250 of 1954 would become the make's most widespread model until its closing in 1959.
It made 12 hp at 5,300 rpm, weighed 395 lbs. and reached 75 mph. Its oscillating rear suspension was equipped with an upper anchor system,
like the Velocettes, at a time when sliding rear suspension, given rigid frames, was still in use. This FR also introduced
a new and very Japanese gadget, a gearshift indicator, with five ring-shaped lights on the headlamp.*

At the same time, the number of manufacturers did not stop growing. Japan nineteen which had different makes of motorbike in 1945, counted forty-two by 1952 and eighty-three by 1953. There would be one hundred and fourteen in 1959. But these were mostly small, regional manufacturers and competition was intense. Production, which had trebled in 1951, then 1952, and which again doubled in 1953, braked a little in 1954. From initial enthusiasm, there followed a "hangover" effect. While the automobile was "beyond" average household means, the unbridled rivalry certainly stimulated innovation and progress, but purchasing power remained limited. Only the strongest would survive this mad scramble.

The commercial structure became essential as Honda understood before anybody else. Promotion through racing took on vital importance, and it was indeed the

The unknowns of the 1950s

At the start of the 1950s, as before the war, it was the British influence which prevailed, and a string of small makes went into building machines from 90 to 250 cc, absolutely worthy of their models. A major part of these makes would let go of Anglomania for Germanomania during the 1950s, and only a small élite would survive beyond this decade. Abe Star, which started off in pre-war Tokyo with 350 and 500 cc models, is a fine example from this period. They were in production from 1950 to 1957, during which the obvious English influence was overtaken by an unquestionable originality. After a 150 cc two-stroke, the make returned to four-strokes in 1951 with a 150 rocker-valve mono with refined exhaust, looking no different alongside a Triumph Cub. There followed a 350 twin-cylinder V, very exclusive and forward leaning, and in 1957 a new single-cylinder 350 which dared a forward engine block which the make only dropped to return to separated gearboxes for its final models in 1959.

A poster of the first Tokyo Motor Show: automobiles, motorbikes and commercial vehicles.

future big names of the 1960s, and they alone, who would shine in the various events already written into the sporting calendar. The customer had become an "informed sportsman" who, would no longer be buying no matter what. On the other hand, exports were still negligible ; one thousand two- and three-wheelers left Japan in 1956, and only two thousand four hundred and forty-six in 1957.

Copycats !

This would not last because the famous MITI, the influential Ministry of International Trade and Industry, was created in 1949 to replace the Ministry of Trade and Industry (notice the nuance). American Occupation officially came to an end in April 1952 (in fact, twenty-eight thousand G I s would still be stationed at Okinawa in 2000) and the MITI recom-

A short-lived curiosity, this is the 225cc Kongo agricultural and commercial machine, made by the Fuji Kikai Manufacturing in 1955 in an attempt to bring together the functions of both vehicle and stationary engine. The side-valve single-cylinder engine was pressured-cooled by air and a winch could be jaw-clutched to the hub of the rear wheel.

The year after their establishment in Tokyo in 1950, the firm Sumita Hatsudoki ("Sumita Engines") commercialized a 150 cc rocker-valve twin-exhaust single, looking very British, but which was not merely a pure copy. It was joined in 1952 by this 200cc. Type 2C which claimed 3.5 hp, 200 lb, and 56 mph. Until their disappearance in 1955, Sumita would go on to produce an entire series of models from 90 to 250 cc based on the same concept.

This 125 Emuro ED100 of 1958 is typical of the Japanese school of the period. Before going out of business in 1961, the make would also produce a two-stroke 500 twin prefiguring the Suzuki T500 of 1967.

mended as of 1952 the introduction of new technologies to Japan, with the declared aim of improving local products and making them suitable for export. Following this advice to the letter, the majority of young makes at this time were influenced shamelessly by Europe. To the conservatives, who continued to copy the English, came the modernists inspired by the Germans. The second would be counted among the survivors. And naturally, these technological imitations took part most of the time while flaunting the rules of industrial courtesy, without even consulting the original manufacturers.

This make located at Misima, a little town between Tokyo and Hamamatsu, entered motorbike manufacturing in 1950, and until its disappearance in 1956 would be one of the pioneers of overhead-valve four-strokes. The range was made up of 140 then 150 cc luxury models (with vertical cylinder and twin exhausts) or "Sport" like this 1953 single exhaust model, with inclined cylinders, external flywheel and four-speed gearbox, weighing in at 175 lbs.

Cabton : English myth with Japanese sauce

Cabton (in distorted English "Cammand by to Osaka Nagakawa", the initials of which compose the make's name) started up in the middle of the 1930s with a very British-looking 350 cc (using, however, a single-cylinder side-valve Indian engine). This was followed by a superb rocker-valve 500 which had the lines of the Swiss MAG engines, then well known in Japan. Throughout its existence, Cabton, always very influenced by Europe, remained faithful to the British concept of the motorbike, with relatively powerful singles and twins, sometimes marketed under the Mizuho label ("land of rice"). Traditional supplier to the police and the army like Meguro and Rikuo, Cabton would still be the sixth major Japanese manufacturer in 1955 (with 9,987 units produced that year), then would sink rapidly, unable to take the corner at the end of the 1950s.

In 1954, Cabton persisted in copying whatever arrived from abroad. This RTS 600 cc twin is a replica of the disastrous Indian Scout which appeared in 1948 and it uses the unusual rods of the external rocker arms. The MJ was a 250 cc single-cylinder replica. Irony of fate, these curious models would be the simultaneous swan song of the copied Indian and of the copier Cabton, which would close down in 1958.

This single-cylinder Cabton 350 RBH of 1954 was influenced by the Ariel Red Hunter. It employs the aluminium cylinder head adopted by Ariel at the start of the 1950s, but keeps a simple cradle frame and sliding rear suspension while Ariel were already into double cradle and oscillating rear suspension. On the same basis, Cabton would also build a side 400cc and a 500 cc that would equip the Imperial Guard in Tokyo (Asama Memorial Cottage document).

BMW emulators

The Japanese really liked copying BMWs, sometimes right up to their tank emblem. So one finds, from 1956, the BIMs, whose name alone was an admission, and the Rikuo 250, and from 1965 to 1968, the 500 cc Lilac R92, ultimate creation of that make. There were also the DSKs (Daito Seiki Company) but here was a case apart because, as of 1954, this Tokyo firm was producing its A25 and A50, copies of the BMW R25 and R 51/3, with the agreement of the German firm with the condition of not exporting to Southern Asia or Europe. DSK even met with good racing results before its factory was destroyed in 1959 by a fire.

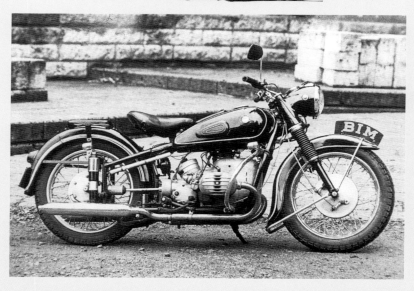

At DSK, they were not content with just copying BMWs. They also thought back to the Scott Sociable of the 1930s, as is witnessed by this astonishing coachwork side-car of 1955. It appears that this machine remained at the project stage and was never marketed (drawing by M. Nakaoki).

The DSK A50 of 1956, perfect copy of the BMW R51/3 of the same period, developed 25 hp for 419 lbs. and 85 mph.

The 500 BIM in 1957 : look for the differences from the contemporary BMW.

Less a copier than it might appear, Rikuo was not, at first, content with being directly influenced by the 250 BMWs and their 68 x 68 mm measurements. The 350, here in its 1954 version, posted measurements of 76 x 76 mm. It developed 16 hp, weighed 375 lbs and made 60 mph.

The man in the picture clearly shows how the dream was still arriving from abroad, but this two-stroke Tsubasa 125 Fighter, with strong Germanic engine shows some very Japanese lines. Its finish and luxurious fitting-out with electric starter did not prevent it from sparkling with 7hp at 7,700 rpm, 256 lbs., and 60 mph.

After the tricycles of the 1930s, Tsubasa gave some time to Anglomania with a rocker-valve 250 much acclaimed in 1954-1955. From the following year, and up until their end in 1960, Tsubasa also gained much inspiration from BMW. Such was the case with this Falcon GC 250 of 1959, which confessed to the same measurements as the BMW (68 x68 mm) but only produced 12 hp for 375 lbs. and 55 mph as against 15 hp, 350 lbs., and 80 mph for the BMW R26 of the same year.

In search of personality

It would, however, be dishonest merely to underline this European influence, so evident at the start of the 1950s. The priority very speedily became to search out a separate identity. And out of the entire range of the big makes, a real Japanese style gradually emerged, offering a unique cachet, typical and steeped in local culture. A major production country had been born and it would soon become Europe's turn to be influenced by Japan.

Japan becomes the lone horseman

This vicious battle, in which a very aggressive and inspired Honda served as dynamo, was totally out of rhythm with the rest of the world. Elsewhere, the motorbike capitulated and its long history faded without protest against an automobile now affordable thanks to the post-war economic boom. In the United States, Indian disappeared and left Harley-Davidson calmly vegetating. In Eastern Europe, the motorbike was more than ever present. In England, the game of mergers finished by wiping out any vitality among the Big Five. In Germany, the small car and the car simply killed off over-sophisticated motorbikes. In France, the Mobylette suffocated the powered two-wheeler and in Spain, the industry was yet to be born. Only Italy held

The Tsubasa HC 125 Fighter of 1959 stood out by its original casing and above all a sophisticated bike-frame, with an oscillating arm in stamped steel, articulated beside the transmission gearwheel to ensure constant chain tension.

Under strong Germanic influence during their six years of existence from 1952 to 1958, Hurricane was a make of the Fuji Group, which also made Rabbit scooters. Its production included single-cylinder 350s then rocker-valve 250s and two-stroke 125s. This 125 RK 21 of 1956 stands out with its curved-back exhaust, exactly like those on the German TWNs.

Compact, neat, and practical, the 50cc Cub Type F would enable Soichiro Honda to invest in the production of more sophisticated motorbikes. Legend has it that the round gas tank of the Cub F was in fact a water-heater which the money-saving Fujisawa had bought up in bulk.

accessible with a simple license and authorized riding the 250cc with a favorable permit.

In spite of everything, under pressure from strong competition, those makers incapable of making real changes and those neglecting the lower powered range, in placing everything on technical beauty, would be swept away. Through this formidable shortcut, in only a dozen years, the history of the Japanese motorbike caught up with what had taken Europe over half a century.

The purge was merciless : the Tokyo Motor Show that welcomed over eighty manufacturers in 1955, only housed twenty-eight by 1957, and those vegetating with an output under fifteen thousand units per year were condemned.

on, without getting involved in exports and above all thanks to customs barriers.

The motorbike triumphs from an absentee car

This protectionism reduced the automotive market, held at 44.6 % by foreign cars in 1951, to no more than 8.9 % by 1955. The reflex "buy Japanese" was working to the full, especially as importation was also severely controlled. Japan was importing no more than three or four hundred powered two-wheelers per year between 1955 and 1960, essentially for evaluation by the builders and not for resale.

The Japanese motorbike had two great advantages during this period : the absence of popular light cars like those already around in Europe, and a simplified driving permit which from 1955 made the 125 cc

Following on from the 150cc Pearls, Portlys, and Showas of 1953, then the 200 and 250 Hosks of 1954, Honda arrived at the overhead camshaft in May 1955. Sadly, they had still not mastered this technique. The SA looked all of its 377 lbs. (20 more than its rocker-valve rivals) and contented itself with 11 hp (against 12 or 13 for the rocker-arms and 16 for the two-stroke Suzuki twin of 1956). It was nevertheless the most expensive after the Liner twin. Honda would re-adjust their aim.

The big makes of the time
Honda : the small subsidizes the big

One often forgets that, in his journey towards the top, Honda did not merely content himself with inventing the modern motorbike. From 1955, it was the low-powered, less expensive models which ensured the major monetary returns necessary for the development of prestige models such as the 250/350 overhead camshaft machines. To this end, in 1952, the Model F "Cub" came out, essentially a 50 cc auxiliary engine fixed onto the rear wheel of a bicycle. With this hardy machine, Honda became the national market leader in 1953 and 1954. The factory built up to seven thousand of these in November 1952, 70 % of the entire national output for that month !

Honda would understand very early on that production is nothing if not followed up by sales promotion ; they would be the first to go abroad, the first to export to the United States (in September 1954) and the first to offer a one-year guarantee (in February 1956). They would also appreciate that a healthy business organization was essential (offering shares on

Without a doubt, a real Japanese style had been born and arrived at its peak with the Honda Dream CS71 of 1958, a 250cc (54 x 54 mm) rigged as a scrambler, developed from the C70 of the previous year.
There is an anecdote that Soichiro Honda, depressed by the difference in performance between his racing machines and those of the European manufacturers, was at the time deeply into mysticism and that these "Cs" followed the lines of a typical Shinto temple. Their specifications still make one dream : 18 hp at 7,400 rpm, a simple chain-driven ACT, 16-inch tires, 348 lbs., and 75 mph, not forgetting an electric starter, the first of its kind.

Better than the Ford Model T or the famous Beetle, the Honda 50cc Super Cub! Exported from 1959 into the United States, it has since been seen in one hundred and twenty countries around the world. Its little four-stroke horizontal engine, which would become a Honda classic, was linked to a three-speed semi-automatic gearbox and fixed into a U-shaped frame in stamped steel. It weighed 155 lbs. and accelerated to 35 mph.

January 1954 marks the birth of the first Honda scooter, the Juno K. Its engineering came from the Dream E (189 cc, 6.5 hp, three-speed gearbox), but the bodywork was partially created in polyester and fiberglass. Heavy, not very efficient and costly, the Juno K suffered most of all from a disastrous unreliability. The engine overheated under the bodywork, which itself systematically cracked.

the Tokyo Stock Market in January 1954) and that to seriously fine-tune their machines would demand the building of their own test track (in May 1958). They would especially take into account that top-range models (like their first twin-cylinder, the C70 of September 1957) would only be justified if mass-production justified this luxury. And the 50 cc Super Cub C100 of August 1958 would prove the most brilliant and most long-lasting example.

This brilliant machine, half-scooter, half-moped with semi-automatic transmission, passed beyond the twenty million manufactured mark in March 1992, so becoming the most produced transport machine in the world.

In the meantime, it would guarantee Honda huge returns for over thirty years.

And it was with such "general public" success that Honda managed to swallow certain bitter setbacks, like that of the Juno K scooter of 1954.

Tohatsu : surprise leader in 1955

The origins of Tohatsu (short for Tokyo Hatsudoki, or "Tokyo Engine Factory") go back to 1922, when the company began by building railway trucks and then small generators. These little engines would be most useful immediately post-war, enabling Honda and others to power their first motorbikes.

Tohatsu went into two-wheelers in 1949 and, somewhat by chance, found themselves market leader in Japan during 1955 with an output of 45,267 machines. Their industrial structure was already relatively powerful, their range reasonable and well in tune with the period, and Tohatsu therefore made sure, fleetingly, of bridging the gap between the "scooter generation" (Rabbit and Pigeon) and the Honda steamroller.

This success was short-lived. Tohatsu was still second in 1956 and 1957, but hungry young enterprises soon began to bring out better developed two strokes. Tohatsu, a conservative business, neglected its sports models and racing scarcely ever smiled on it. In a Japan that, at that time only swore by the Honda CB72 versus Yamaha YDS1 duel, this was crippling. As a result of a strike, Tohatsu would abandon the motorbike at the start of 1964 after a belated attempt to link up with Showa in 1959. The majority of their technicians went over to Bridgestone.

In 1958, Tohatsu was offering no less than four different 125s, all based on the eternal copy of the DKW engine with its 52 x 58 mm measurements. The LA, here posing in front of the magnificent Mount Fuji, innovated with a distinctly modern, tubby design, a stamped steel frame on which was hung a new, inclined-cylinder engine (with unchanged measurements) and a dynastart starter.

The lowered-powered Tohatsu models had been renowned for their performance and the Runpet 50 of 1962-1963, offered in three versions, could reach 6.8 hp at 10,800 rpm and 60 mph with the sports kit form. A range of accessories also enabled it to be transformed in a scrambler.
(Asama Memorial Cottage document)

The beautiful Tohatsu 125 LD, twin-cylinder two-stroke brought out in 1963 would the make's swan song. It was perfectly representative of the fashion and technology of the period, with its squared engine (43 x 43 mm) boosted by twin carburetors and producing 12 hp at 7,300 rpm. Starting was by dynastart and the published performance was tempting : 71 mph or 19 seconds for a standing start 400 meters. (Asama Memorial Cottage document)

The twin-cylinder Tohatsu 125 LR would be British champion in the hands of Dave Simmonds in 1963. Attaching value to supplying racing motorbikes to private riders, Tohatsu also offered a 250 cross.

For racing, three Tohatsus are worth mentioning, beginning with two competition-customer machines. The 50 Runpet, born in 1961, gave some great moments to numerous private entry riders, in particular finishing third and fourth in the 1962 United States GP (outside the World Championship). As for the 125 LR twin of 1963, this would enable Dave Simmonds to become British Champion.

The most interesting racing Tohatsu remains the air-cooled 50 twin, available in very small numbers to private riders starting in 1963, and at the handlebars of which Dave Simmonds again excelled. His best international result was ninth place at the 1964 TT : the twins Honda and Suzuki, but also Kreidler and Derbi, were already too strong at this period to allow him to bid for the best results. The bare performances of the little twin were correct, but its all too fickle reliability pushed the majority of "private entries" into favoring the Honda CR110. Tohatsu is today well known for its outboard engines, its pumps, and its portable generators.

Hosk : trapped by technical nobility

Yamarin had been importing European and American motorbikes since the beginning of the century, but only created a manufacturing arm in 1946 with the goal of building motorcycle engines. With this aim, the firm took on technicians previously with Nakajima : an authentic reference point ! Unveiled in 1949, the first complete motorbike introduced overhead camshaft technology (chain-driven) into Japan.

In 1953, Yamarin motorbikes adopted the Hosk label, with an OHC 200, then a 250cc evocative of the German Horex, followed by 125 and 250 two-strokes influenced by the German TWNs. In 1956, came a new series of single-cylinder rocker-valve versions from 250 to 500 cc, again reminiscent of Horex. But it was above all with its prestigious twin-cylinder 500 cc of 1955 that Hosk came to be known. The engineering was Triumph-inspired, in the shape of the low engine, the con-rodding keyed to 360°, the dimensions 63 x 80 mm like the first Speed Twin, and the Burman-

In 1926, Yamaha-Rinseikwan was importing (among other makes) the British Ariels. Becoming a manufacturer several decades later under the Hosk make, Yamarin remained faithful to its origins and would shamelessly employ this line drawing on their leaflets copied from an Ariel advertisement.

Unfortunately, this avant-garde "SH" machine also proved rather capricious. The average dealer, still recruited from bicycle salesmen, lacked experience with such sophisticated engineering and still did not know how to put it back on its stand.

To rectify this poor reputation, in 1954 Showa launched their Cruiser, which created the opposite effect : this side-valve 250 was heavy and lacked elegance, even if its backbone frame and its oscillating forks were still little used in Japan. The Cruiser quickly became a great commercial success in Japan, its reliability redeeming its mediocre performance.

style separated gearbox with right-hand shift. Hosk had just perfected their model by adding an overhead camshaft with lateral chain-drive, and one of the most modern double cradle frames, with oscillating arms in sheet metal. Here was the most hi-performance machine on the Japanese market for its time.

Alas, this fine engineering and all too restricted distribution led to this make being taken over by Showa in 1959. From now on, Yamarin decided it was financially preferable to go into import-export.

Showa : the most beautiful Japanese make ?

Showa was born in 1939 but only really began to produce motorbikes in 1946. From the start, this make showed themselves technically very advanced and wasted no time in ensuring a place for themselves on the local scene. Only local, because their personnel, extremely young and creative, were more concerned with technology than with business and neglected setting-up a real national network.

On the other hand, their sporting successes ensured a flattering reputation. The victory of their 150 SH (whose overhead camshaft engine was supplied by Hosk) at the Nagoya TT in March 1953 was an exceptional event. This race, the first post-war large scale trial, created a considerable stir.

This Showa SG 150 of 1953 hid its cards well. Under its neat look and classical curves, was a very interesting little overhead camshaft engine developing 6 hp at 5,000 rpm. Its bike-frame was also very avant-garde with its oscillating rear suspension.

In 1956, and following Yamaha's success, Showa went over to two-strokes, like so many others. However, their Light Cruiser was not just ordinary ; it introduced an induction exhaust valve only to be rediscovered on Yamahas in 1971. As for the Cruiser SC of 1958, separate lubrication singled her out, without doubt a first for Japan (others would get there in 1964). Finally, the 125, which took part at Asama in 1959, innovated a rotary distributor like the one on the East German MZs, a principal which Suzuki would only adopt in 1962 !

In 1959, Showa took over Hosk and linked up with Tohatsu for the manufacture of the Echo moped and the Pandra scooter. Everything seemed to be going well : the range was wide and the image strong. Showa, however, wanted to do too much with ruinous prototypes and even with a midget car. The make was then employing one hundred and thirty engineers, while even Honda counted only two hundred. Sales stagnated and the firm met with big cash flow problems. They ended up by being swallowed up by Yamaha in April 1960. Yoshio Kojima (boss for 32 years !) had lost the struggle.

The legacy would not be entirely wasted : the advanced research on two-strokes at Showa would be quickly exploited by Yamaha, notably the rotary feeder which would re-appear as from 1961 on the 125 YA-5. As for

The 250 SC Cruiser 57 of 1957 justifies the astonishing shape of its engine (and of its about-turn exhaust) by its side valves. Its modest 10 hp pushed its 340 lbs. to almost 60 mph. Nothing very thrilling, but just what was wanted in Japan at that time. (Asama Memorial Cottage document)

Strange evolution : Showa passed successively from overhead camshaft to side valves then to two-strokes. No matter, this very typical 250 Cruiser SCT of 1958 redeemed itself by offering separated lubrication, 15 hp at 5,500 rpm, and 75 mph. Observe also that during this period the standard versions of Japanese motorbikes were most often single-seaters.

2サイクル単気筒・ダイナスターター付   125CC

ライトクルーザーSL Ⅲ

Showa's last and maddest dreams appeared in 1956 at the Tokyo Motor Show in the guise of an extraordinary 350 with a two-stroke horizontal twin engine. Unfortunately, the reality would be duller and Showa would make their last profits from motorbikes like this 125 SLIII of 1958, a luxurious commercial vehicle that nevertheless reached 56 mph.

the ex-Showa engineer, Hatta, he would create some of Yamaha's most beautiful Grand Prix machines of the 1960s. And Hosk's final project would be reborn in 1969 by name of... Yamaha 650 XS-1 !

Liner : too elitist

Affiliated to the Kitagawa Group, Liner got going in 1952 as the Portly make with a small, chain-drive OHV 150 cc. This model was immediately followed by a 175 cc with rocker valves, with Portly immediately taking their place along the top ten national manufacturers.

On the other hand, from 1954 the make made no progress and fell back to twelfth place ; rivalry was already harsh and by letting go of inexpensive machines, Liner wanted to follow the road to sophistication for a still fluctuating market, that of beautiful motorbikes. In particular, in 1954, they launched their 250 TW, an almost identical copy of the 500 Sunbeam S8. Not only did the choice of model prove inadvisable (this longitudinal twin was one of the "prettiest" technical failures of the British firm) but once again, the make deprived itself of the "fat" from the market, with a machine that was too noble and too expensive to produce.

Liner persisted, and in 1955 out came a 125 inspired by the NSUs of the time. This choice can be justified, since Honda had also done this—but with one slight difference ; alongside these hi-performance machines, Honda was also building a large quantity of very simple motorbikes. The Liner factory, particularly well equipped with machine tools (and notably in gear-cutters), ended up being absorbed by Yamaha in March 1959.

The Liner TW 250 is a 250cc replica of the 500 Sunbeam S8. With a history of making things worse for themselves, Liner launched this model with a rocker feed and 9hp, before going over to the simple ACT, to reach 12 then 13.5 hp at 6,000 rpm. Alongside this, the bike-frame abandoned its telescopic front suspension linked to a sliding rear one in favor of oscillating front and rear suspension. The third and last rehash of the TW in 1957, claimed 75 mph despite its increased weight of 350 lbs.

Before turning towards sophistication with their Liners, Kitagawa Manufacturing began in 1952 by producing this little 45 mph, 150 cc.

Suzuki : a serious make

Suzuki, a family firm specializing in the textile industry (like Toyota in the beginning) went into popular vehicles manufacturing in June 1952. It was, after all, only another way of using metal. The first model was called Power Free, and was a two-stroke 36cc bolted into a bicycle. This engineering had a feature special to other auxiliary engines at the time—it was equipped with a free wheel that stopped the machine from stalling at the back. Its success was underlined at a rally linking Sapporo to Kagoshima, nine hundred miles over eighteen days.

In May 1954, Suzuki went still further with its Colleda CO, a complete motorbike with a four-stroke 90 cc engine. And this novelty, in turn, also proved successful in competition by winning its category in the second running of the Mount Fuji race. The same year, the 50 cc Mini-Free was introduced and was soon known as the most popular in the maker's range. The SM1 Suzumoped of 1958 was the model that put the make

Rare reunion in front of the Suzuki museum at Hamamatsu, the three mopeds or cycles with auxiliary engines that marked the beginnings of the make. At the back, the first Bicycle Power Free E1 of 1952 with its adaptable 36 cc, 13-lb. engine. On the left, the Diamond Free of 1953 which gave 60cc, 3.2 hp, two speeds, and a telescopic front suspension for thirty-eight thousand yen. On the right, a more developed 50 cc with engine block and belt transmission, the Mini Free2 of 1957.

into orbit, a solid second place behind Honda. For all this, Suzuki did not sacrifice the top end of their range that was developing in all its aspects. As of March 1955, the Cox appeared, a 125 cc version of the CO, as did the ST, another 125 but with a two-stroke engine. Suzuki devoted its greatest attention to the latter, putting it through an endurance trial of ten thousand kilometers prior to production. It was from such meticulous care brought to the tuning of its models that Suzuki's good reputation quickly spread across the whole of Japan.

From 1955, the make came in eighth among national manufacturers and was fifth by 1956. With such success, Suzuki made a great hit that year in launching the 250 TT, the first mass-produced two-stroke twin with IMC. Not content with being first, Suzuki confirmed themselves in this class as one of the most durable

For forty-five thousand yen, a Japanese in 1958 could present himself with this Suzumoped, a 50 cc, much more elegant than the MF 3 big bike powered by the same little two-stroke engine, and which only cost twenty-three thousand five hundred yen the same year, largely thanks to Suzuki's first stamped steel frame.

The 100 Suzuki Porter Free of 1955, in a most commercial version, at the service of a travelling musician.

Street scene in Japan, with a Suzuki Colleda CO of 1954 on the right .

Priced at 235,000 yen, the twin-cylinder Suzuki TT of 1956 was the most expensive for its output, but was far and away the most powerful, with its 16 hp at 6,000 rpm that powered its 348 lbs. to 80 mph. The Honda ME could only claim 14 hp at that time and the Yamaha YD-1 still did not put out more than 14.5 hp in 1957. One would have to wait for the Honda C70 of 1957 and its 18 hp before Suzuki would really find a competitor up to its stature. Observe the horseshoe-shaped headlamp which appeared for the first time and became one of the make's distinguishing characteristics, as well as the rather bizarre carrier.

The first Yamaha YA1 of 1955 poses in front of a music store.

references in terms of power and reliability. The tradition of these two-stroke twins is still alive today.

It is noticeable how at the start Suzuki kept a low profile behind their models (Diamond Free, Power Free etc.) and hid behind the acronym SJK (For Suzuki Jodosha Kogyo, Suzuki Automobile Manufacturing) or again under the label Colleda (transcription of "Kore-da" : "it's that one").

The business would only become the Suzuki Motor Co. Ltd., with the famous stylized "S", in October 1958.

Yamaha : a meteoric rise

Well known for musical instruments since the end of the nineteenth century, Yamaha became involved with the motorbike in 1955 ; the tooling used in airplane propeller manufacture during the war enabled them to take up this activity with relative guideness.

The chosen model was a fairly faithful copy of the DKW RT 12, out in 1949, with the exception of the transmission : the gearbox had four speeds instead of three and gear transmission replaced primary chain drive. Complicity between allies conquered and humiliated by a war going back only a decade was toned down but profound.

It certainly appears that Yamaha engineers went over to learn from DKW at this period and that they returned with a know-how about two-strokes that Suzuki would not master until seven years later when borrowing it from MZ.

The links between Yamaha and Auto-Union, underground as they might be, were in any case long-lasting and even if only by chance, even today, the two manufacturers in the world of mass-produced five side-valve engines are Yamaha and Audi.

The 125 YA-1 had however nothing exceptional

alongside the countless 125s which proliferated on the Japanese market in 1955. At 138,000 yen, it was even more expensive than its rivals, with the exception of the Hosk, which was even more powerful (6.5 hp instead of 5.6). No, what made the difference was

Yamaha's aggression on the sporting scene, and notably a remarkable overall result at Mount Fuji and Mount Asama. Only just born, but thanks more to an excellent team preparation than its intrinsic qualities, the YA-1 made fools out of the other 125s.

A group of 250 YD-1s here on trials before being launched in the market, accompanied in the background by an Asama-type 125 YA-1 with raised exhaust.

Baptised the "Acatombo" (Red dragonfly), the YA-1 immediately encountered success thanks to its reliability and racing success. This first Yamaha was an improved copy of the DKW RT 125, with a difference in size: its gearbox included a fourth speed.

In 1956 Yamaha was placed twelfth in national sales while their range was limited to this single model and to the 127 and 175 cc models.

In three years, eleven thousand and eighty-eight examples of the YA-1 left the factory, an exceptional figure for a very competitive market, and one which can be put down to two other factors : the fine manufacturing quality of the machine (its prototypes were put through ten thousand kilometres of trials, the big boss himself taking the handlebars for an incident-free journey from Hamamatsu to Tokyo) and a particularly elegant line. The YA-1 is in fact one of the first motorbikes whose decoration (specially in the livery) had been entrusted to a specialized office, GK Design, which has since designed the majority of Yamahas.

From their beginnings, Yamaha considered themselves as challengers.

As much as Honda and Suzuki would for a long time show proof of a definite solidarity (the first, for example, would lend their test track to the second until they had built their own) so Yamaha would always be confronting Suzuki and above all Honda.

This was an attitude notably linked to the personality of the founder, Genichi Kawakami, a feudal "old school" patron, whose personality (except where authority and competence were concerned) was in every respect contrary to that of Soichiro Honda.

We shall see just to what extremes such a rugged opposition would lead the two opponents a quarter of a century later.

Great rival to the CB 72 Honda, this 250 Yamaha YDS-1 was the dream of all the young Japanese in 1959-1960. Its 20 hp and its 333 lbs. furnished it with a top speed of 85 mph. The CB72 would smother any on-road rivalry just like in racing.

Yamaha's early offerings were successful, and its first two-stroke twin-cylinder, inspired by the German Adler, arrived perfectly in tune with the market in 1957. Certainly this YD-1 was less powerful than the Suzuki, but it was also less expensive and more elegant (1.5 hp, 70 mph, and 185,000 yen against 18 hp, 80 mph, and 195,000 yen for the Suzuki TP of the same year). A fierce rivalry would for a long time go on between the 250 twins from the two makes.

Following pages :
With their Version B of 1956, the YA-1 passed from 5.6 hp to 6.8 hp and reached 50 mph. It only remained to give it a more marked identity. No sooner said than done, with this YA-2 of 1957 whose design, as with that of the 250YD1, was entrusted to a design office in Tokyo : GK Design.

Pointer : from the four to the two-stroke

Pointer was the business label of the firm Kirin, part of the big industrial Shin Meiwa group, even today involved with engineering and metallurgy. Kawanishi, famous for its aircraft, also belongs to this group. And like so many other aircraft firms, once peace had returned, Shin Meiwa went into motorbikes.

The Pointer story began in 1947 with the PD model, a little 56 cc engine inversely mounted into a bicycle frame, a curious configuration that would be taken up by other manufacturers.

The following year, a side-valve 150cc appeared, then a rocker-valve in 1950. The first 250, in 1952, was an English-style single cylinder rocker-valve (68 x 68 mm) with a separate gearbox, with right-hand shift, coming up with 11.7 hp, 330 lbs. and 50 mph. Its ultimate 1958 version which featured an original design and an Earles fork boasted 12hp and 60 mph. Their pretty, well-developed four-strokes were not slow to build up a fine sporting reputation, and during the mid-1950s, Pointer was regularly placed among the ten biggest Japanese manufacturers, with a peak of 15,496 machines in 1953 and over 46,000 motorbikes sold from 1952 to 1956.

But the era of the two-stroke had arrived and followed the trend set by Suzuki in 1956. It was Pointer's turn to market a top-of-the-range 250 twin-cylinder in 1957, at the same time as Yamaha, DNB, and IMC. As with

One may search in vain for the English or German influence in this 125 Pointer Bike Let of 1960 with its 17-inch wheels, one of the most individual and original attempts of its time. This two-stroke-engined hybrid scooter (9 hp, 4 gears, 285 lbs. and 55 mph) would be very short-lived and would unfortunately not enable Pointer to establish themselves alongside their all too powerful rivals. (Asama Memorial Cottage document)

British influence remains obvious on this Pointer Ace 250 PA-4 of 1954 and comparison with later models shows just how rapid the Japanese revolution had been. Observe on the crash bar of this 250 the retractable arrowhead indicators as on the 203 Peugeot.

The Pointer 175 PCB 11 of 1958 was a motorbike very typical of the end of the 1950s, with its undeniable German influence (the measurements were still those of the DKW engine) linked to an increasingly Japanese style. This type of pendulum front fork was a Pointer feature.

Hesitating between two tendencies, the Pointer 250 PA-T of 1957 opted for a compromise, with two aluminium hubcaps on the mudguard supports to give an appearance of the Earles-type telescopic fork.

the 125s, the inspiration came from Germany ; the Suzuki TPs, Yamaha YD-1s and Pointer PA-Ts, all copied from the Adler, shared the same dimensions 54 x 54 mm. Producing 15hp at 6000 rpm, 364 lb., and 70 mph, the Pointer was distinguished by its tubular and pressed steel structure, but did not keep the kickstart and the coaxial gearshift of its inspiration.

Unfortunately it would not have the same glorious line of descent as the Yamahas and the Suzukis. Pointer proved unable to take the exportation corner and abandoned the motorbike for good in 1963.

Their last and sumptuous burst of energy in 1962 was their first racing 125, a two-stroke twin, whose lines were reminiscent, even molded on, those of the famous Itom 50.

Meanwhile the make would favor us with a certain number of 125s and 175s completely representative of the period.

Meguro : grandeur and decadence

Meguro very opportunely went into motorbikes in 1937 to take advantage of Army orders. Their first machine, the Z97, was a 500cc rocker-valve, very influenced by the Swiss Motosacoche (including its 82 x 94 mm dimensions) and would survive until the end of the 1950s.

Having started off with high power, Meguro developed their post-war range with beautiful and very English-looking 250 and 350 rocker-valve single-cylinder models, but also with hi-performance twins.

Riding high on commercial success, they launched a rocker-valve 125 in 1955 and flanked their twin-cylinder

Appearing in 1937, the single-cylinder Meguro 500 remained popular until the very end of the 1950s. On this Z6 version of 1955 with its sliding suspension, observe the streamlined headlamp and the blinkers, as yet unknown in Europe.

500 with a 650. At last in 1958 Meguro attempted to free themselves from British influence and to exploit the sporting image of the victorious Mount Asama prototype by launching the 125 E3, 250 F, then 350 YA with their simple overhead camshaft. Too heavy, lacking flair and kick, these elegant motorbikes would meet with such little success that Meguro soon returned to rocker-valve models.

Despite some clumsy choices, Meguro still held their own with the top ten Japanese manufacturers until 1960, but decline was imminent. That year, Meguro signed an initial agreement with Kawasaki, to completely disappear by November 1962.

Kawasaki themselves adopted the average-powered singles (the Estrella was the real descendant) and until the 1970s, their 650 W1 and W2 would be the direct heirs of the Meguro big twins.

The Meguro 250 of 1956 was the medium-powered four-stroke typical of its period. Competitively, one could clearly be more modern and above all more efficient than its 10 hp and its 400 lbs. It would not be long before Meguro lost ground.

The 500 K1 of 1961 remains a prestigous top range model for Meguro, at a period when the young makes were levelling out at 300 cc. It was one of the most efficient machines on the Japanese market, and its K2 development would in 1965 be the final motorbike to carry the Meguro marque.

Hamamatsu, cradle of the japanese motorbike

Hamamatsu and Daytona have two points in common : a vast beach with regular breezes and a certain love story with the motorbike. The similarities stop there. Nevertheless…
if Honda, Suzuki, Liner and Lilac all originate in Hamamatsu, if Yamaha comes from Shizuoka (several miles to the east), if Showa's roots are in Numazu (again a little further east), this is not by chance.

First of all, Hamamatsu possesses a long sporting history : its beach has always been the venue for formidable kite-flying combats, as is witnessed at a superb museum downtown. The annual reunion of these splendid flying machines is the most important in Japan, and draws a considerable crowd.

Next, the region has a solid image of competence in the matter of manual work. Its labor, at any time, has gone into working in wood and then metal. Four of today's biggest model specialists (Tamiya, Hasegawa, Fujimi and Aoshima) are based in Shizuoka, and several musical instrument makers like Kawai and Yamaha are to be found along a stretch of only a few kilometers.

A taste for competition (in Japan, kite-flying is a very serious business that for several centuries has been contested by highly trained teams), skilled labor, but also a crisis in the textile industry (well developed in the region)—and it did not need much more for a young and dynamic industry such as the motorbike to develop. Noticeably, not a single automobile make, or even the "older" motorbike firms, emerged from this region : all originated from Tokyo, Kobe, Nagoya, Osaka, or Hiroshima, traditional industrial centers.

In 1968 Kawasaki would make this rocker-valve 650 W2 (here in its TT scrambler version), as heir to the Meguro twins. Indicative of its old-style conception : the four-speed gearbox, separate from the engine, was still controlled by the right foot. This machine producing 53 hp, like the overhead camshaft Yamaha XS-1, would remain in the catalogue until 1975.

The 250 S8 of 1962 was a key model : the fuel tank still carried the Meguro label but the engine was already stamped "Kawasaki".

The symbol of Mount Asama

At the start of the 1950s, the heightened rivalry among the countless Japanese makes found its natural extension in competition. An initial 233 km race, contested at Nagoya on March 21st, 1953, brought together nineteen manufacturers. It saw victory for N. Kanebo on an overhead camshaft 150 cc Showa, ahead of a 150 Honda Dream 3E, a Liner, another Dream and a Monarch. The over-restricted and slow course (about 30 mph average) would not be used again.

The official Yamaha team at the start of the 125 race during the first running of the Mount Asama event. The YA-1s were still close to production models.

Another event was organized on Mount Fuji on July 12th. This 10-mile hillclimb course, although not particularly interesting, attracted ninety-nine entrants. Victory went to a certain Nagoaka, on an Auto-Bit 90, ahead of a Monarch. This race, reserved for dealers, was revived in 1954 (with wins by a 90 Suzuki CO and a 250 Monarch), in 1955 (125 Yamaha and 250 Honda) and 1956 (125 and 175 Yamaha).

In February 1954, Honda sent an official team to race at Interlagos, near Sao Paolo. The race was quite sophisticated, won by Nello Pagani, the 1949 World Champion on his Mondial. Although Michio Omura finished thirteenth and last in the 125cc class riding a standard Dream, the event made a definite impact in Brazil as in Japan. To the extent that Honda boldly announced that, in five years' time, he would race in the Isle of Man Tourist Trophy, the most prestigious contest in the world. At the time, this risky prediction made people think him mad.

Moving on to more serious matters

It was only in 1955 that the first Mount Asama trial was organized. Located 60 miles west of Tokyo, this volcano-extinct for two centuries—rises to a height of 8,300 feet. It is encircled by a majestic mountain range, a real tourist attraction. The circuit takes in 12 miles and demands studded tires : not a single stretch was paved, the track being entirely covered with black ashes. As for regulations, machines that were not 100 % Japanese were excluded.

Despite the cold climate, the first running on November 5th, 1955, was clearly successful : 81 machines were entered, of which 38 directly by nineteen different factories, and 52 were ranked. On Saturday, the big surprise came with the very latest Yamaha YA-1s, which took the first four places in 125, ahead of three Suzukis. The first Hondas (blown Benly JCs) came ninth and tenth behind a modest Lilac Baby.

In reality, the Yamahas did not greatly excel in pure performance, but the factory had taken care to prepare

Michio Omura on his 350 Honda SB-Z, did his best to negotiate the impaved road over which the machines were racing on Mount Asama in 1955.

The Monarch firm was created at the start of the 1950s by a certain Nomura, still a motorbike merchant in Tokyo. The make was also identifiable by this 250 F1, very influenced by the Velocettes, and particularly powerful since in 1954 it won the big Mount Fuji event. The firm would disappear in 1957, unable to reach a real cruising speed due to its low horsepower. This 250 only produced 13.5 hp for 330 lbs., but this was still enough at the time to obtain good results at national races. (Document Asama Memorial Cottage)

very seriously for the event, by arriving at the venue well before the rival teams to check out the course and fuel settings in particular.

In "250", it was a shaft transmission Lilac SY which established itself in the hands of a very young Fumio Ito (16 years old), ahead of a Honda SA-Z. This SA-Z was a single, adapted from a standard SA to developed 18 hp. A Pointer completed the podium.

The following day, Honda consoled himself in the 350 Class, where no other factory was seriously entered. The factory had five SE-Zs in the first five places. In 500, victory for their SD-Z (an SB-Z single boosted to 382 cc) ahead of two DSKs, a Meguro single and three Cabetons, was the most significant.

To improve the breed

The habit was formed. After open-road racing had been banned, including Mount Fuji, the manufacturers' union initiated the building of a permanent track (although still covered with ashes) on the barren sides of Mount Asama, which would serve as a test circuit for all the makes, like Brooklands in England. The site had the advantage of being situated on "neutral ground", and therefore favored no one regional manufacturer. This track was unfortunately not ready for 1956, even though rules were tighter. Each factory would still have the right to five motorbikes per class, but was not able to enter more than two machines of the same type. It was therefore a matter of diversifying the techniques used and of accelerating the technology ; Asama was

Masuko races ahead of Sunako and Shimoyoshi, all riding 250 Yamaha YDs, during the 1957 event. The first two would move on to auto racing, the first with Mitsubishi and the second with Prince.

trade event whose clear aim was the improvement of the breed. Some would play the game (different bore/stroke ratios from Yamaha), others less so : Honda, always the rebellious, were content to differentiate their prototypes by their carburetors, which already created tension. On the 19th and 20th October 1957, twenty-eight machines representing no more than seven manufacturers came to the starting line. On a

During the 250 race in 1957 a Honda C70-Z leads Sunako's Yamaha.

At the start of the 1957 race, Soichiro Honda himself poses with the armada of machines that he has entered for the event. Numbers 2 and 104 are 305 cc C75-Z twins, while Numbers 6, 7, and 109 are 350 SB-Z singles.

circuit whose development had been reduced to 5.843 miles, Yamaha repeated their feat in 125 : Oishi (on the 54 x 54 mm YA-A) beat Miyashiro (on a 56 x 50 mm YA-B), completing the twelve laps at over 54 mph average ! They were ahead of two Honda C80-Z twins (a little too experimental with their five-speed gearboxes and their 16-inch rear wheel) and a Suzuki RB. The Suzuki factory was not officially represented, and if the Honda was the most powerful, the Yamaha had the better road-holding.

It was also the hat-trick for Yamaha in 250, since Masuko (on a 54 x 54 mm YD-a) came in ahead of two 56 x 50 mm YD-Bs. Yamaha beat four Honda C70-Zs, but at a lower average to that of the 125s, which were definitely the supreme class. Five Hondas won in the 350 class (two C75-Z, 305 cc, twins and three SB-Z singles) in front of a Hosk. Finally it was two singles, overhead camshaft prototype Meguro RZs, which made their presence felt in 500. Meguro also gained second, fourth and fifth places, only a Hosk managing to place itself between them in third place. The Meguros, painted in aggressive yellow, had just returned from a victorious tour in Brazil.

It's war !

During this second running, differences of opinion cropped up between the participants. Some, like Honda, wanted to make this race into an inter-factory confrontation, their preserve, the exclusive showcase for their technology. Others, like Yamaha, preferred to open up the trial to any rider and even to foreign makes so as to better gauge their international level. It was with this aim that in the spring of 1958 Yamaha entered an official team in a race on Catalina Island, offshore from Los Angeles, California. Fumio Ito came sixth in this event.

For 1958, the organizers therefore subdivided each cubic capacity into two categories : one for the factories, the other in the "clubman" format, accessible to all amateurs on non-standard machines. Although they also moved the race forwards to August 24th, this did not prevent it being run under a real downpour of rain ! Three Hondas made their impact in 125 "factory", and five Yamahas took the top five places in 125 open... at exactly the same average speed (but over two laps instead of three !) Honda won both categories in 250, but only just, in the open class, ahead of two Adlers, a Showa, and a Monarch.

The 350 "private entries" fell to a BSA Gold Star ridden by the young T. Takahashi (17 years old). Later on he

If the production Meguros were rather quaint, the prototype RZ 500 cc entered in 1957 at Asama was, to say the least, advanced with its overhead camshaft.

would become Honda works, would be the first Japanese to win a Grand Prix in 1961 and would achieve a long and brilliant career on four wheels.

Having driven for Tyrell in 1977, as late as 1995 he would even finish eighth in the Le Mans 24 Hour race !

For the moment, he came in ahead of a 260 Yamaha YE-1, while the Honda 305 twins scored a hat-trick in the factory class.

In the absence of official Japanese 500 machines, it was a Triumph twin which took this capacity ahead of a

Two American riders had taken part in Catalina in May 1958 alongside Fumio Ito on the 250 YD-A. The result was not famous, but the machines remained in California where Cal Rayborn went on to obtain some fine results for the half-mile.

A 250 Showa Cruiser takes off from one of the countless bumps which punctuated the Mount Asama course.

In 1959, a large crowd watches the start of the 125. The Hondas are leading already.

BSA, a Hosk, and two BSAs. Finally an unlimited race was organized where two Triumph 650s led Takahashi's BSA (making a mad recovery), two Honda 305s, a Yamaha 250 and a BMW R69 600. The winner, American Bill Hunt, would be recruited by Honda when the factory entered Grand Prix racing.

The beginning of the end

The schism occurred in 1959 and a breakaway club (the MCFAJ) organised their own race on April 19th. Two Yamahas won the 125 ahead of a Honda, a Honda came in ahead of two Yamahas in 250 and a 500 Norton dominated both a Honda 350 and a Yamaha 260 in the "over 250".

The usual meeting itself took place from the 22nd to the of 24th August… in the absence of Yamaha who, of course, was boycotting this meeting as too professional to his liking. Out of the three hundred and nineteen entries, forty-five were works riders, and forty thousand spectators had assembled down the sides of the volcano!

In the "amateur" class, Honda made a clean sweep of the 50 cc (with five Super Cubs!), of the 125 cc (with four C90s), of the 200 cc, and even the 250 cc ahead of a Yamaha.

In 350, Noguchi, on a Yamaha beat four Hondas; the factory would later send him into Grand Prix racing. Takahashi (BSA) pocketed the 500 ahead of four other BSAs, two BSA A10s were ahead of three Triumphs in the "over 500", and a BSA 650 won the "unlimited" in front of another BSA, a Honda CR76 and Two Yamaha YDSs. This domination by the large capacity BSAs prompted Meguro to launch their K1 in 1960, a 500 copied from the very British BSA A7.

Sadao Shimazaki, future winner of the final Mount Asama event, poses before the race behind his Honda RC 160. This four-cylinder machine with its twin overhead camshaft and four valves per cylinder put out 35 hp at 14,000 rpm and reached speeds of 125 mph. Shimazaki would later become one of the high-tech testers for Honda, notably when the make first entered Formul One.

The turning point of the 250 race : Noguchi and his Yamaha YDS-1R goes inside G. Suzuki and his Honda RC 160 during the seventh lap of the event.

On the works side, in Yamaha's absence, it was a very young private entry by name of Kitano, on a Honda SS 92, who dominated in 125 ahead of the three official RC 142s, only just returned from the Isle of Man Tourist Trophy.

Kunimitsu Takahashi (left) and Fumio Ito (right) congratulating each other at the finish of their crazy duel in 1959. They would later meet up again in Grand Prix, the former with Honda, the latter with Yamaha.

Kenjiro Tanaka appears satisfied with his performance at the finish of the 250 race in 1959, with his mechanic and his RC 160. Honda would send him off to race in Grand Prix during the 1960s, just like his namesake Teisuke Tanaka.

They were followed by a Suzuki RB and two Tohatsu twins. Kitano would be quickly signed up by Honda to race in Grand Prix.

In 250, the key event, Honda entered the first Japanese four-cylinder machine in history. This RC 160 showed real menace and not surprisingly gained the first three places at an average of almost 66 mph. A CR71 twin was fourth, another RC 160 was fifth.

The latest Lilac Lancer V-twins were left behind and the brave attempt of Noguchi's private entry Yamaha would be in vain ; its transmission failed while he was battling for third place.

Noguchi would have his revenge the following day in 350, ahead of a Honda CR76. As for the 500, this was the occasion for a fabulous duel between R. Ito on the BMW R50 and Takahashi on the BSA Gold Star.

The former won at an average of close to 70 mph, even faster than the four-cylinder Honda 250s. Behind them came a BSA A7, an OHC Showa-Hosk twin (Showa had just taken over Hosk) and another BSA. Ito, already victor in 250 in 1955, would go racing privately in Europe in 1960 with a BMW RS, and then become Yamaha works rider, winning several Grand Prix.

The return of nostalgia

Because of tensions between manufacturers, this would be the last time that Asama was organized. Honda was already taking part in Grand Prix, followed by Suzuki in 1960 and Yamaha in 1961. Asama, having served its purpose as spring-board was abandoned in favor of a more structured Japanese championship, raced on paved roads better adapted to the performances of modern machines.

In November 1962, Honda organized at Suzuka, on their own brand new circuit, the first Japanese Grand Prix, which would become part of the World Championship starting the following year. The Mount Asama circuit, would be taken over by automobile manufacturers, who would turn it into a test track for their rally cars. Motocross would also be raced there.

Several years ago, a handful of enthusiasts wanted to leave some tribute to this heroic age of the Japanese motorbike. These enthusiasts built a museum at the race site, called the Asama Memorial Cottage. And their Asama Meeting Club, which is deliberately limited to one thousand members, organizes twice a year, in May and October, a reunion-contest-exchange market on the car park in front of the museum.

World expansion

In the 1950s, Japan partly owed its growth to a relatively low standard of living for individuals while the country and its businesses became rich. From 1955 to 1965, the average income was multiplied by three and a half while the cost of cars was divided by two, but the Japanese remained frugal : "overconsumption" was for tomorrow, and the forty-eight-hour week was still in force in 1960.

Honda was being imported into France beginning in June 1961 and their CB92 caused concern, with its 15 hp at an incredible 10,500 rpm. However, it was hard for buyers not to dream given its futuristic lines, and even more, its specifications : 80 mph, brakes worthy of a 500, overhead camshaft, electric starter, and red saddle never before seen, especially, on a 125 cc. At the same time, the state-of-the-art French motorbike was the Terrot 125 Tenor, which featured only 7.6 small horses, rocker-valves, and almost 60 mph. It was, however, far less expensive : 1,750 FF against 3,040 FF for the Honda.

The standard of living did, however, go up for the Japanese. In 1960 the government announced a plan to double incomes during the next ten years, and this would be respected : the monthly salary at Honda, of 23,400 yen in 1959, would go up to 49,200 yen in 1969. Consequently, whereas in 1960 there was one private car to every 240 inhabitants (or a vehicle, whatever it might be, to 68.7 people), this ratio grew in 1970 to one car to every 12 inhabitants (or a vehicle to every 5.9 people).

This was still far removed from the American ratio (one car to every 2.7 inhabitants in 1965) or even the French (one car to every 6 inhabitants in 1965). But for the moment, this progress in the standard of living was at least turning the Japanese away from scooters and towards real motorbikes. Starting in 1955, Pigeon and Rabbit left Honda and Tohatsu to fight it out for the two top places in the national market, with Suzuki ranking second in 1958.

The motorbike for everyone

While the European motorbike started to cross the wilderness and put itself on the fringes as a machine either totally commercial or blatantly sporting (and therefore necessarily dirty and fragile), the Japanese invented leisure-motorbiking, reliable and clean.

Above all, the Japanese manufacturers recognized the virtues of marketing. They would from now on be producing those motorbikes demanded by the market and not (like the westerners) those which they deemed it wise to propose based on their own criteria. Even if it meant abandoning the promising "Japanese school", stemming from the progressive German school, in favor of a conservative American school, made of gimmicks and chrome. In this respect, the Honda CB 72 of 1960 was typical, in so far as it marked an about-turn

A pretty mountain road (the Japanese landscape is superb), three buddies, and a Suzuki 250 TB for the luckiest among them : an almost common sight in 1962.

Following pages : The 250 Honda CB 72 was the joy of young Japanese sportsmen. This one was fitted out with YPS special parts of the time (saddle, remote controls).

Classical, homogenous, and balanced, the 250 CB 72 launched at the end of 1960 would seduce the whole world and establish itself as a big commercial success. It was therefore the right choice, despite already very American lines, bristling with chromium-plating. Its characteristics would create a sensation in Europe : 180° inclined twin, 24 hp at 8,000 rpm, 337 lbs., and 95 mph. Here is its 305cc version the CB 77.

Everything has a beginning: it was at the wheel of this van that, around 1965, Jean-Claude Olivier, then a very young Yamaha importer for France, would win over his first customers with these demonstration motorbikes.

when compared to the C71 of 1958. It was Japanese style pragmatism, even if this CB 72 innovated a con-rod assembly wedged at 180°.

Exportation, a necessity

The Japanese soil does not contain any particular richness. From time immemorial, the sea and paddy fields have nourished the Japanese, but the land, very wooded, is unproductive. The territory, three-quarters of which is mountainous, is almost inaccessible and a large part is uninhabitable. Two-thirds of the 125 million Japanese are concentrated on a coastal strip of land which joins Tokyo to Kobe, or just 3 % of the territory or scarcely 10,000 square km. Very dependant on importation where raw materials and energy are concerned, Japan can only count on a conversion industry. She is therefore condemned to export to survive as she was condemned to expansion during the period of the pre-economic wars in the pro-birth Meiji era.

Revenge on America

When exports really took off in 1957, the first market targeted was the Americas (the United States but also Brazil), for reasons of closeness as well as maturity : the leisure civilization in the United States was already

underway and, from 1960, 60 % of the imported motorbikes were of Japanese origin.

Europe came later. If the 1959 Amsterdam Motor Show was flattered by the presence of a Honda stand, the first Suzukis and then Hondas only arrived in France in 1961, followed by Yamahas in 1962, Bridgestones in 1964, and Kawasakis in 1967. One would even see a few belated Lilac R 92s. Besides it was only in 1962 that exports really shot up, even if France during that year only took in 654 Japanese machines… of which 501 were mopeds !

Two imperative watchwords

Two priorities became of capital importance : diversification and exportation. This was because the home market was saturated. The number of powered two-wheelers on the road stayed at between eight and nine million between 1966 and 1976. The automobile was becoming more powerful and light cars (the K-cars or midgets, suggested from 1955 by the MITI and practically introduced in 1960) were invasive : Suzuki turned to the automobile in 1955, Fuji-Subaru in 1958, Mitsubishi went back to it in 1965 with the complicity of Toyota and the Mitsui Group (bank, commerce), which was their common origin.

For diversification, Honda had once again played the pioneers : their first auxiliary engine, for agricultural use, dates from October 1953. As for exportation, this was even more crucial since protectionism remained severe (34 % import tax), competition was tough, and the performance-obsessed customer only bought the machines which he had seen winning races, in Japan or abroad. It was in allowing sport and competition to pass them by that a firm as powerful as Tohatsu had to pull out in 1963, while it was thanks to their race results, in commercializing real "competition-customer" machines (CR-71 and YDS-R in 1959, then TD-1A in 1962) that Honda and Yamaha would succeed.

So it was by leaning excessively on exportation that Japan overtook France as the world's top motorbike

Following page, below : Pretty symbol of the turning point of the period : this sample from the 1960 Suzuki range brings together, from right to left, the 50 Selped, the 125 Seltwin and its 150 scrambler version, the 250 Twinace and the Suzulight TL light car.

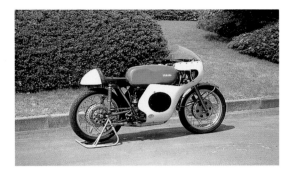

The Honda-Yamaha duel was rife from the 1960s with the raceworthy versions of the C71s and YDS-1s.
Yamaha drove the point home in 1962 with the first representative of the TD generation.

manufacturer in 1960, and overtook Germany as the top exporter in 1962. In August 1961, Honda produced over one hundred thousand powered two-wheelers in one month, a record for the world motorcycle industry. Exportation was not however everything. Honda and Suzuki established themselves in Taiwan in 1961, Yamaha in India in 1963, and Honda set up in Belgium in 1962. Relocation was only just beginning.

Sweeping away the competition

Alongside the leaders, numerous overcautious, quaint and over-passionate makes were wiped off the map. Monarch had disappeared in 1957, Emuro and Cabton in 1958, Rikuo and Tsubasa in 1960, Showa absorbed Hosk in 1959, and was in turn swallowed up by Yamaha (just like Liner and Queen Rocket) in 1960. Kawasaki digested Meihatsu in 1960 then did the same with Meguro. Pointer and Olympus (no relation to the

The Queen Rocket 125F of 1959 developed 7.8 hp, but this over-calm and reasonable model would the last from the make. (Asama Memorial Cottage document)

Definitely tempted by exotic solutions, in 1957 Olympus launched this 250 crown type H with flat-twin shaft transmission. This East-German replica of the MZ-IFA 350 presented a attractive power of 15 hp and promised 72 mph (drawing M Nakaoki).

cameras of the same name) closed their accounts in 1962, Yamaguchi in 1963, Tohatsu in 1964. IMC (Itoh Motor Company) had started up in 1947 under the Hayafusa make with a little 80 cc two-stroke. Founded by a defector from Mitsubishi, the make had then produced a long series of little side or rocker valve 150-175 cc models. IMC would first of all use Mitsubishi or Cabton engines, then, in 1955, the 250cc rocker-valve KH1, one of the very first engines produced (almost fourteen hundred units) by Kawasaki. IMC would then launch their own two-stroke engineering, out of which a 250 twin which would be one of the first of its type in 1956. Severely damaged in a typhoon, the factory had to close down in 1961 and was finally absorbed by Nissan Diesel in 1962. As for FMC (Fuji Motor Company, no relation to the Fuji Sangyo of Rabbit scooter fame) and the Itagaki Group (Sunlight manufacturer), it was not long before they threw in the towel machines, but they totally missed the export boat. And yet, at the end of 1964, Honda alone held 62 % of the American market.

Having started off in the middle of the 1950s with 250s and 350s influenced by German machines, Olympus quickly became the spearhead for the Japanese school, but not for long. One still recalls with nostalgia their 250s and 370s with their curious egg-shaped tank, presented respectively in 1960 and 1962. The 250 shown here, powered by a Rumi-type two-stroke twin, featuring 21 hp, 340 lbs., and 95 mph and was made in very limited numbers. The 370cc, built on the same basis, counted three cylinders in line, which doubtless makes it the first motorbike of this type in Japan, if not in the world. It would unfortunately remain at the developmental stage. (drawing M Nakaoki)

By 1960 a really local style, innovative and individual, existed in Japan, as represented by this FMC Gasuden type BES, a 125 two-stroke twin in similar guise as the contemproary Suzuki. It produced 11 hp. and 60 mph. (drawing M Nakaoki)

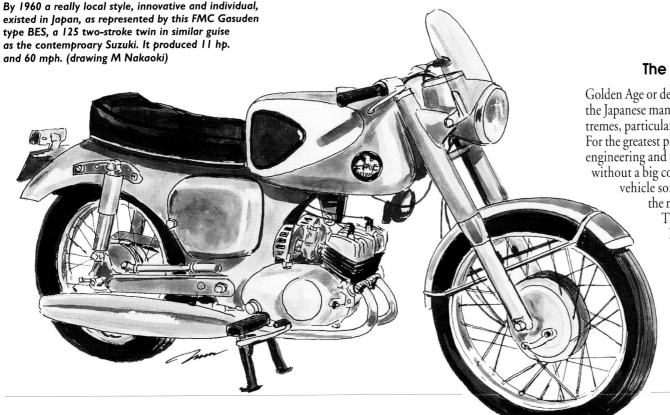

The extreme scooters

Golden Age or decline ? The start of the 1960s pushed the Japanese manufacturers to the most wonderful extremes, particularly where the scooter was concerned. For the greatest pleasure of both those in love with fine engineering and collectors (but, it must be admitted, without a big commercial success), this commercial vehicle sometimes rose to the most costly and the most sophisticated technology.

The 125 Honda M80 that came out in November 1960 contrasted sharply with all the other scooters of the time, be it for its flat twin-cylinder four-stroke engine or its Badalini-type semi-automatic hydrostatic transmission. Revised as the 170 cc M85, this lavish machine did not meet with the success that should have justified its remarkable conception.

The forward-mounted flat twin engine gave the Honda M85 scooter a perfect balance. This beautiful engineer's dream nevertheless proved too sophisticated, too costly, too heavy (322 lb.) and would not bring in the projected success.

The 125 Silver Pigeon C-140 (or 143cc C-240) of 1963 gave the lie to Mitsubishi's reputation for conservatism with regard to Fuji's Rabbits. Its lines were more American than natural, with is curvaceous chrome-plating, and its engineering was distinguished by a pretty little two-stroke twin.

A point in common for these two marvels : a price fluctuating between 145,000 and 169,000 yen, at a period when the "midgets" (these latest 3-meter-long, 360 cc light cars) offered four places in the warm and dry for three hundred thousand yen. The customer did not hesitate.

Yamaha's faux pas

Honda had almost gone down in 1954 because of their Juno K scooter and it was also a scooter's fault that brought Yamaha a hair's breadth away from bankruptcy in 1961.

The 175 Yamaha SC-1 of March 1960 was this make's first scooter. It was particularly elegant and its technology was daring (hydraulic converter, hydraulic rear brake), but Yamaha had marketed it before it had been perfectly set up. This adventure, costly in both after-sales service and in reputation, would led the make to the brink of failure.

It should be said that at the same time, Yamaha was taking part in Grand Prix racing and that its expenses were excessive in relation to the firm's stature, which was only just producing two-thirds of Suzuki's output. Yamaha's situation became so critical that this young make, having only just entered the World Championships, was obliged to pull out in 1962. This was because the MF-1 moped came out at the same time as the SC-1 scooter. It was also technologically bold : body frame in pressed steel, rear-spring suspension countersunk in a rubber block, centrifugal gearshift, electric starter. Yamaha spared no expense in competing with the all-powerful Honda Super Cub. Alas, the fine-tuning was just as sloppy as that of the SC-1 and Yamaha, who had been heavily relying on these two models, were temporarily forced to mark time.

Serious claimant in the race towards sophistication among the big factories, the Mitsubishi C-140 contented itself with a conventional transmission system, but offered, in return, a two-stroke twin engine.

The MF-1 moped, second consecutive blunder for Yamaha after the SC-1, lead the firm to a hair's breadth away from throwing in the towel. The elegance of their lines and their advanced technology deserved better.

Initially planned as a 125 cc, but too labored, the magnificent Yamaha SC-1 scooter with hydraulic converter transmission would be increased to 175cc at the last moment. Out of this came all its troubles, with the congenital fragility of its under-powered two-stroke single.

It was the ordinary and common 75 YG-1 of March 1963 that brought the make out of its rut. This model would meet with a good commercial career (specially in its separate lubrication version of 1964). It would put Yamaha back on the road to growth, under the drive of Hisao Koike, appointed director in May 1962 having previously been in the "musical instruments" division.

Some new arrivals get talked about

Kawasaki, iron fist in velvet glove

Kawasaki, established in heavy metallurgy since the beginning of the century, had been building aircraft since 1924. From 1949, the firm entered into the development and then the commercialization of engines adaptable for motorbikes. This concerned simultaneously a 60 cc two-stroke and a 150-250 cc four-stroke developed using a technology from BMW, a firm with which Kawasaki had been carrying on technical relations since their aeronautical beginnings. In 1954 Kawasaki entered

The secrets of Japanese reliability…

As with the American motorbike in the 1910s and 1920s, the Japanese motorbike established itself as an export thanks to its reliability. It was the same for the automobile industry : in 1956, a team from Toyota was invited over to reorganize quality control at Buick !

As for this reliability, the Japanese auto and motorbike had acquired it at home, on universally potholed roads : In 1956 ; 2 % of the road network was blacktopped (17 % of the country's roads) ; in 1964, still less than 4 % ; in 1975 still less than one third and, in 1982, only just over half ! In the 1960s and 1970s, road-building, financed by heavy vehicle taxes, made up over 40 % of the national budget for civil engineering.

The state of the local highway network at least offered one advantage : it demanded sturdy manufacture (at least stable for high speeds !) and in addition, it at first favored the two wheeler at the expense of the automobile. In 1995, 73 % of the Japanese highways and roads had been blacktopped… compared with 92 % of the French network, even though considered very rural for Europe.

… and several other characteristics

Other aspects particular to the Japanese market had in turn slowed down its progress in exportation. The fact, for example, that the transport of a passenger had for a long time been forbidden, in particular on the highways, had damagingly led the manufacturers to neglect this aspect of practical motorcycling. In the same way, the great public safety which reigned in Japan had discouraged manufacturers from concerning themselves with developing efficient anti-theft devices.

One of the first appearances of Kawasaki under their own name, at the International Export Show, at Osaka in 1960. Until then, the 250 twin had only existed under the Meihatsu name.

into the production of complete machines, under the label of a subsidiary named Meihatsu, and even tried their luck by putting their own name on a few scooters. It was only in 1960 that Kawasaki decided to seriously involve themselves in the motorbike, "killing off" the Meihatsu make, establishing their own factory for low-powered machines, then buying up Meguro, the senior make, king of the four-strokes. Kawasaki soon went past the critical output figure of ten or fifteen thousand per year, putting many makes in danger and so becoming, starting in1965, the steady fourth major manufacturer in the country. Taking advantage of their own experience like that of Meguro, their range became one of the most complete on the market, from the very latest 650 twin-cylinder designed after the Meguro 500 to the 50 cc moped-scooter, with the 125 and 83 cc approach was different to that of the three other major manufacturers. Geographically installed in "Kansai" to the west of the country, near to Kobe, this business had a completely specific attitude of mind.

To generalize, one might say that the people of Kansai were both Southerners and the historic lords of Japan, whence a curious mix of warmth (without going too far) and of traditionalism (which does not mean conservative).

It was under their own name that Kawasaki Aircraft launched this scooter in 1954. Scarcely two hundred examples would be built before the make understood that yt couldn't compete with two giants in the forms of the Fuji Rabbit and the Mitsubishi Silver Pigeon.

The very first Meihatsu 125 had been marketed from 1955 to 1957, successively with a rigid frame, then with a sliding rear suspension and finally an oscillating version. Its 125 cc two-stroke engine (53 x 56 mm) was an entirely original realization by Kawasaki Aircraft and did not appear to have been copied from anything else, which was particularly common for Japan at that time.

In addition, Kawasaki skilfully carried on this difference, regularly playing the mavericks and the independence card with their three competitors.

Lilac, the make that could have taken on Honda

Originally from Hamamatsu like Honda, Lilac might have met with the same destiny. In addition, its founder, Masashi Ito, had started off as an apprentice to Soichiro Honda with whom he shared a passion for engineering. Ito started up his own make in 1948, but unluckily, he always lacked an associate manager and moderating influence like Fujisawa.

His 90 Baby of 1953 is really typical : At Lilac, even the most basic commercial vehicles had to be sophisticated and in particular to have shaft transmission. Very efficient for its class, the Baby's positive success in 1955 encouraged Ito to pursue this path and invest heavily. And he wasn't completely wrong : the victory of his 250 ST single at Asama in November 1955 assured him of an enviable prestige.

Lilac, however, had neglected the 50 cc commercial vehicle niche which would make their competitors' fortune. Sales stagnated, and they were even shrinking in 1957-1958 before the superb 125s and 250 V-twins came out on the road in 1959. As beautiful as they were efficient, these Lilacs, inspired by the Küchen-engined

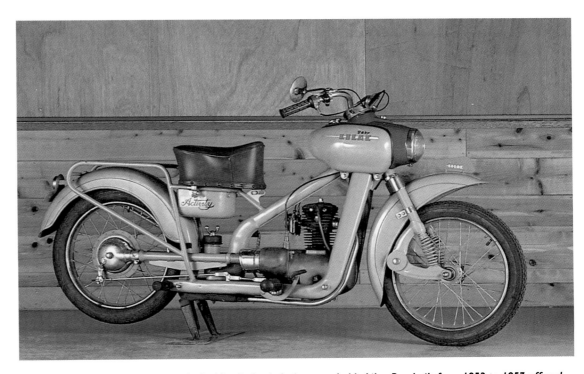

Contemporary and competitive with the Honda Benly J, the remarkable Lilac Bay built from 1953 to 1957 offered a more commercial approach. Its 90cc rocker valve engine had the same measurements of 48 x 49 mm and almost the same performance (3.5 hp and 45 mph). Lilac asserted their individuality with a twin cradle frame, a single shock-absorbing oscillating suspension, two twistgrip speeds, as well as a shaft transmission which would until the end remain one of the make's permanent features. (Asama Memorial Cottage document)

From 1954 to 1958, Lilac were finding their way in life and successively committed themselves to BMW-style singles, from 125 to 250cc, like this 1955 250 SY.

With their shaft transmission, Lilacs were costly to make. The 125 BT was no exception : at 138,000 yen, it was in 1957 the most expensive 125 on the market.

Shaft transmission pioneer in Japan, Lilac started with a side-valve 125, joined as of 1951 by the 150 cc rocker-valve M series. The same year a sports model was born, the 150 KD, which abandoned the rigid stamped steel frame for a tubular twin-cradle with sliding rear suspension. This KD already touched 55 mph.

Victoria Bergmeisters out in 1952, were considered among the most advanced motorbikes of the time from both the technical and the aesthetic points of view. In addition they had a great success in Japan, but their manufacturing costs were prohibitive and they never yielded a sufficiently high return. The height of bad luck, a badly pierced feed fault with the three hundred 250 cc LS18s imported into Holland, led to problems of lubrication and brought vague desires of importing Lilacs into Europe to an abrupt halt.

Then, at last, Ito invested heavily in a new factory for building 50 cc s, but the project fell behind, and ended

Here is the culmination: within the remarkable series of V-twin Lancers, one of the most beautiful motorbikes in history was born. The 300 cc MF 39 of 1959 was quickly followed by the superb 350 cc LS 38, two models that would prove both the success and the ruin of Lilac at the same time. This rocker-valve 250 cc would be rated at 18.5 hp at 7,500 rpm and 80 mph. The series of V-twins would come to an end in 1965 with a final 350 cc version.

No half-measure, the 125 Lilac Lancer V-twin four-stroke, born in 1955, was as sophisticated as the 250. With an 11.5 hp engine was elegantly suspended from its frame, and it reached 70 mph. This CF 40 versions dates from 1962. (Asama Memorial Cottage document)

up lacking the necessary funds. There was talk of negotiations with Suzuki, whose main bank (Daiwa) was the same as that of Lilac, and of really wanting to grasp the know-how for four-strokes. But Ito did not wish to betray his old comrade Honda for one of his competitors. The idea came up of a take-over by Mitsubishi, as bankers were becoming increasingly important at

Lilac chose to invest in the flat-twin starting in 1963, with a very beautiful and original little 125 cc with suspended engine (which would remain in prototype form) and with this more ordinary R92, a 500 very influenced by the BMWs that would be built until 1968. The final version would benefit from an electric starter.

One might swear that this Lilac TW 350 of 1954 was a Douglas Dragonfly. Though noble, it was too expensive for Japan at the time. (drawing M. Nakaoki)

flat-twin. Already, in 1954, they had introduced (with great success) a Dragon 350 of the same design, inspired by Douglas. The 500 R 92 would meet with a modest success in the United States but, conceived in haste, would encounter several problems of reliability and Lilac would have to close down for good in 1967. Completely absorbed by Mitsubishi, the Lilac firm no longer survives today except in the name of a car of this make : Lancer.

Lilacs would sometimes be marketed under the Marusho label, notably in the United States, but the lilac was a favorite flower of Mrs. Ito. Scrupulously honest, Masashi Ito made it a point of honor to pay back all his creditors and to harm his employees as little as possible. He is today living with his wife in a modest flat in Hamamatsu.

M. Hayashi, the engineer responsible for the Lancers, would work for Bridgestone and then on the Honda Gold-Wing project !

Honda. The little 50 cc Lilac imitation-scooter would indeed be marketed under the Silver Pigeon label, but the finance agreement would not materialize and in October 1961 bankruptcy was declared. Soon afterwards, Ito managed to negotiate subcontracting for Honda and having regained the confidence of financiers with equal enthusiasm, he relaunched his business in 1963. Alas, Lilac, which had shined so much by its originality and the quality of its products, this time went to the opposite extreme with a BMW-style 500

Bridgestone : from tires to tires

This firm had been founded in 1933 by Soichiro Ishibashi to manufacture tires. Even the origin of its name is amusing : the translation of "Ishibashi" in English is "stone bridge". We may never know why these two words were reversed.

Under this brand name came bicycles in 1946, auxiliary engines in 1952, and complete machines starting in 1958. The first machines were little 50 cc commercial

Very modest: the first 50 Bridgestone Type 41 of 1958. Its engineering appears to have come from the automobile manufacturer Prince. (Asama Memorial Cottage document)

The 175 TA-1 from Bridgestone in 1965 was the most advanced in its class, but it was a capacity already left behind in favor of the 125s and 250s. With its 177 cc, it produced 20 hp which drove its 271 lbs. to 85 mph.

The Bridgestone 90 EA-1 was an important model. In 1964, the 90cc class became the object of hotly contested races in which Bridgestone became the king. It came in various versions, tourism or sports, the latter (with characteristic rear mudguard) posting 8.8 hp and speeds of over 60 mph.

units. From 1964, the 90 EA-1 had a rotary feeder and posted up several sporting claims that subsequent twin-cylinders (175 TA-1 and 350 GTR and GTO) only backed up.

The firm was well advanced in the metallurgy field, notably for cylinder lining. In 1965 it became the first to adopt chromium-based inner treatment by wire explosion instead of electrolytic solution. Nor should we forget that the TA-1 was the first standard twin-cylinder to adopt rotary feeders, one year before the Kawasakis, even though Suzuki and Yamaha had given

The Bridgestone 350 GTR (road) and GTO (scrambler), exhibited at the London Show in September 1967 were later than the Kawasakis in the same format but their technology was more advanced: dry clutch, six-speed gearbox and rear suspension adjustable by moving around the superior anchor point of the shock absorbers.

When introduced, Bridgestone's 50 twin-cylinder EJR-11 was already less powerful than the Hondas and Suzukis. Its career would be very modest.

up this sophisticated technique for mass production. When in 1970 Bridgestone went back to its original activity, tire manufacture, numerous technicians went over to Kawasaki, the only surviving manufacturer in the region. Despite somewhat high production costs (linked to the technical worth of their machines) and despite heavy investment required for setting up in the United States, Bridgestone had been in good health : in 1966, with an output of around fifty thousand machines, they had a stature only just inferior to that of Kawasaki.

But rumor had it that the banks had been encouraging Bridgestone to leave the way clear for the Big Four, to whom the firm was also supplying tires. Above all it seems that Bridgestone had neglected the four-stroke

This machine only just merits being called a Bridgestone : the likeness is very slim. Its Grand Prix results at least gave the make some free publicity, welcome, but too late.

strategy, a fatal mistake in the United States at the end of the 1960s. Let alone Honda, Yamaha then had their XS-1, Kawasaki their W1, although Suzuki lost much ground in remaining faithful to the two-stroke.

In racing, three Bridgestones are worthy of note : the 90 single, the 50 twin and the 125 twin, all with rotary feed. The first did not look like much, with its simple pressed steel frame, but was the most competitive machine in its class, both on the road and for competition-customer in a very contested cubic capacity in Japan at the time.

The second was derived from the Tohatsu, but with liquid cooling. It had a really short career. This began in March 1966 with a win in the Mount Fuji Grand Prix, then took part in the Dutch Grand Prix at Assen,

Morishita finishing sixth behind the two Hondas and three works Suzukis. At the end of the season, the Japanese Grand Prix enabled Robb, Findlay, and Morishita to place fifth, sixth and seventh, behind four Suzukis, but this was sadly the last public appearance of these little machines, not competitive enough when up against the Hondas and the Suzukis.

The case of the 125 was stranger. In 1972, the Dutchmen, Schurgers and Van Kessel, converted a 175 cc road model into a liquid-cooled racing 125, installed into a bike-frame close to those of the Kreidler Van Been 50s.

Called a Bridgestone (even though the factory was not involved), this machine achieved several fine Grand Prix results, such as a win at the 1973 Belgium Grand Prix. This special one would reappear with different names, like Condor, until the end of the 1970s.

From the end of the 1950s to the end of the make in 1964, the Yamaguchi 50 would one of the most sought-after mopeds. These two late versions are the Autopet of 1963 (below) and the SPB Sort with raised exhaust of 1962, which produced 48 hp and 50 mph.

Yamaguchi crosses back over the Pacific

In the transitional period of the 1960s, one Japanese manufacturer about to throw in the towel found a kindred spirit on the other side of the Pacific Ocean who would take on their output.

Sixth Japanese manufacturer in 1956 and 1957, Yamaguchi let themselves be overwhelmed at the time when they ought to have made exportation a priority. The make was finally forced to stop manufacture in April 1963 after its boss, S. Yamaguchi, had blown his fortune (and doubtless that of his factory) to become a political deputy ! In Japan as in Europe, before any returns, politics starts off by costing money.

His American importer, Pacific Basin Trading Company (or Pabatco), had distributed five thousand machines in two years. Unable to abandon such an activity, they relaunched production with the help of Yamaguchi's engine supplier, Hodaka. The machines, made in Nagoya in an enlarged Hodaka factory, would be exported and distributed uniquely onto the American market from 1964 to the end of the 1970s.

If this example is unique, one must however keep in mind that other manufacturers would for a long time be distributed in the United States under "naturalized" makes. Bridgestones, for example, re-appeared in North America under the Rockford label.

Yamaguchi's final reincarnation, the Hodaka was distributed across the United States until the 1970s, like this 125 motocross Dirt Squirt.

Following pages :
The 50 Suzuki twin RK 66, a jewel that developed 17.5 hp at 17,300 rpm, with a 14-speed gearbox. With its aluminium frame, the machine weighed 128 lbs. and was capable of 110 mph. For 1968, the factory was even preparing a three-cylinder that would never be officially presented.

Named "601", this 150 Yamaguchi dates back to 1958. Producing 7,5 hp for 127 kg, it was capable of 85 km/h.

The golden age of the Grand Prix

Honda's modest participation of in the 1959 Tourist Trophy initiated an extraordinary era for Grand Prix, without doubt the richest and the most exciting in its entire history. Around forty Japanese works machines would were regularly taking part every weekend—extremely efficient motorbikes, but as sensitive to tune as to ride, being incredibly technically, complex.

Racing Hondas first appeared in Europe at the 1959 TT. The 125 RC142 still looked very much like an NSU, but it was a twin-cylinder with four valves per cylinder. Its engine was in fact a half-RC160. (drawing M. Nakaoki)

hat was Honda's secret ? Above all, and at the time when the European industry was struggling (NSU and Norton had stopped any development since the end of 1954, Mondial, Gilera and Moto-Guzzi had abandoned Grand Prix at the end of 1957, even MV-Agusta was going to fleetingly suspend their official participation in 1961), Honda invested huge funds to develop ultra-sophisticated engineering.

If their engines looked like the NSUs, they had never less than two cylinders in 125, and four in 250, with four valves per cylinder : unheard of at this period. Capable of astronomical running speeds (14,000 rpm !), these ultra-powerful engines were not always equipped with chassis of the same quality, but no matter : very quickly, their raw power enabled them to widen the gap between the single-cylinder MV-Agustas, MZs and Ducatis. In any case, this first race yielded nothing glorious : Bill Hunt fell and the four Japanese riders were spread out over sixth, seventh, eighth and eleventh places.

1960

At the beginning of the season, three Western riders (one of whom, Bob Brown would meet his death during practice for the German GP) arrived to initially support the Japanese riders entered by Honda. They clinched a few honorable positions, as Redman and Phillis each finished a 250 Grand Prix in a respectable second place with distinctly advanced engineering that hardly resembled the old NSUs any more. Suzuki's modest beginnings were limited (as for Honda the previous year) to only the Tourist Trophy in 125, with a conventional two-stroke twin-cylinder that finished in fifteenth, sixteenth, and eighteenth places.

An impressive row of new Hondas at the trials for the 1960 Tourist Trophy.

The first real racing Suzuki, in 1960, was this 125 RT 60. The 13 horses of its twin-cylinder unit were not enough to challenge the Hondas, MV-Agustas or MZs, which were already enjoying around twenty horsepower. The streamlining, as was customary at this time, was in hand-beaten aluminium.

1961

Honda walked away with almost everything in 125 as in 250, with new European riders attracted by the previous year's performances. There was only Degner, runner-

Tom Phillis on the four-cylinder 250 Honda RC 161 in 1960.

At the start of the 125 French Grand Prix at Clermond-Ferrand in 1961, one identifies on the front line Nogchi (Yamaha N°5), Takahashi (Honda N°3), Hailwood (EMC N°17), Phillis (Honda N°1), Degner (MZ N°9), Redman (Honda N°2), Shepherd (MZ N° 10) and Oishi (Yamaha N°4).

The very first Yamaha entered in Grand Prix, the 125 RA 41 single-cylinder with two rotary feeders, was still a close copy of the 125 Showa. The engineer Hatta had in addition been "bought up" at the same time by this firm. Here is Noguchi starting off in the 1961 French GP.

up World Champion on his MZ, to put a check on the 125 Japanese tidal wave of Phillips (first), Taveri (third), Redman (fourth) and Takahashi (fifth). Without the political complications which prevented him from participating in the final Grand Prix (he was of East German nationality), Degner would have without doubt beaten Phillis. In 250 cc, Hailwood, Phillis, Redman, Takahashi and McIntyre finished in that order. It was a first title for Hailwood, who did not yet have official rider status, but whose obvious talent made him worth the loan of two machines during the season.

As for Suzuki, they came nowhere. Their latest 125 and 250 cc rotary-feed twins were not competitive, despite the efforts of Paddy Driver (seventh in 250 at the Belgium Grand Prix), Frank Perris, and Hugh

At Assen, in 1961, Phillis leads Hailwood in the 125 race. By the end of the season they would be the first two world champions for Honda in 125 and 250.

Anderson. Even at the Singapore Grand Prix, a non-championship event contested in September, the Suzuki 125s only finished second and third behind a Honda.

Yamaha's beginnings were less disastrous than that of their rivals : out of the entire season, the best results were eighth place for Noguchi at the French 125 Grand Prix (its first running) and fourth (and last !) place to Ito at the Argentine 250 Grand Prix. The machines were single and twin respectively, one after the other with two rotary feeders. Basically, they were in fact Showas, modified by Yamaha after taking over this very innovative make.

1962

Honda

A season without a 50 class, but featuring a plenty of champions in 125 like Taveri, Redman, Robb and Takahashi who finished in that order. In 250, Redman and McIntyre made sure of the double, while the participation of a blown 250 in 350 bore fruit with the double for Redman and Robb.

The only shadow that fell on this brilliant season was

In a paddock at the beginning of the 1960s. Soichiro Honda (on the right) converses with his riders K Takahashi (seated) and T. Tanaka (standing).

in the Tourist Trophy : Takahashi was seriously injured and Tom Phillis met his death. There was the glimpse of an arms race with the appearance of a 50 cc twin during the non-Championship Japanese GP, contested in November on Honda's own circuit. Tommy Robb rode it to victory.

Suzuki

The make had taken Degner on at the end of 1961, and their 50 had been transformed by springtime. The German had brought over all the MZ know-how in his baggage and he carried off first place in the 50 cc, ahead of the Kreidlers of Anscheidt and Huberts and Taveri's of Honda. Suzuki was less successful in 125 : Anderson snatched a win in the final Grand Prix in Argentina. In 250, Perris managed a fifth place at Assen with the twin. This would be his only result during the season.

Yamaha

Following financial difficulties, Yamaha was obliged to put Grand Prix behind them for this season. The factory could only find consolation at the end of the year with a third place by Fumio Ito on the new RD 56 in the non-championship Japanese 250 GP.

1963

Honda

Honda, who were already getting involved in the automobile, neglected the development of their racing machines. It also appeared that the numerous accidents of the previous season (serious for Kitano, Takahashi, and K. Tanaka, fatal for McIntyre, Phillis, and Hocking), even though Hondas had not been involved, had momentarily thrown the make's sporting participation into doubt.

In 50 cc, Taveri's twin had been totally swept aside and he had only caught up by winning the Japanese GP at the end of the season.

In 125, the twins of Taveri and Redman were outdated and were replaced for the final Grand Prix by a four-cylinder machine. 250 witnessed Redman's knife-edge victory over Provini's remarkable Morini single : following an incredible sequence of bad luck, the Italian duo won. In 350, it was another championship for Redman, without much opposition.

It would appear that during this year Honda became the first manufacturer to employ electronic ignition. This fact has for a long time been ignored because, externally, the system resembled the normal magneto and Honda did not willingly allow race machines to be photographed. It is however probable that, in this matter, the Japanese equipment manufacturer Kokusan had been ahead of the Spanish firm Femsa, long considered as the pioneers of this technology.

Suzuki

A tightly contested 50 cc season ended up with Anderson's win ahead of Anscheidt's Kreidler. Mitsuo Itoh won the Tourist Trophy, a performance that created a great sensation in Japan.

Also a fine win for Andersen in 125 : this was the first win by a two-stroke in this category. A very modest season in 250, only just relieved by the appearance of a liquid-cooled square four for the final Grand Prix in Japan. Anderson finished ninth, but it was at the controls of this machine that Degner was victim to a terrible fall from which he would never completely recover.

At the 1963 United States Grand Prix, raced at Daytona (outside the World Championship), there was a raid by the Japanese motorbikes: from left to right, here are the winners in the three classes : Mitsuo Itoh (50 Suzuki), Ernst Degner (125 Suzuki) and Fumio Itoh (250 Yamaha). If the first is today still with Suzuki, the second died in 1983 and the third at the start of the 1990s.

Yamaha

The racing budget only permitted participation in three races in Europe, in June and July, and uniquely in 250. Ito's fine riding gained him third in the 250 Championship thanks to a fine win in the Belgian GP and to three second places (in the TT, at Assen and in Japan). One wonders what might have happened had he been able to compete throughout the whole season. Phil Red joined the team for the final GP in Japan, replacing the injured Tony Godfrey. He finished in third place.

1964

Honda

The make boycotted the first Grand Prix, at Daytona, officially because of insufficient start incentives, but in reality because their machines were not ready. In a nail-biting end of season, Ralph Bryans only just missed the 50 cc title ! On the other hand, Taveri and Redman made sure of the double in 125 with their fours. The

250 wasn't worth it compared with the Yamaha, and would be relieved by the fabulous six-cylinder machine for the penultimate Grand Prix in Italy. As for the 350, this was still in the bag because Redman won all eight races in the calendar ! At Assen, Redman became the second rider to win all three categories during the same day (the first was Hailwood at Sachsenring in 1963).

Suzuki

Thanks to Honda's withdrawal in the first event, and to the cancellation of the results of the final race (only five riders took the start), Anderson took the 50 cc title. He only finished third in 125 on an ageing twin. The only results in 250 were Anderson's fifth place in Spain and Bertie Schneider's third place in France. These lukewarm results were linked to Suzuki's occupying a good number of its race technicians throughout the year with the development of the 250 cc T20 road model.

Yamaha

The make banked everything on their 250s and, despite the desertion of Fumio Ito (who would never fully recover from a serious tumble in Malaysia in March), Read won the title ahead of Redman and Shepherd's of

MZ. This was the first time that a two-stroke became world champion in this engine capacity.

A completely new twin-cylinder 125 made its appearance at Assen, finishing second, but was not seen again during the season.

At the end of 1964, there was no longer any jealousy : the three participating Japanese manufacturers had all been rewarded. The Japanese hegemony was established in all its variety : two-stroke for Suzuki and Yamaha ; four-stroke for Honda, with engines of two to six cylinders.

1965

Honda

A fine double for Bryans and Taveri in 50 cc, despite the boycott by Honda at the first Grand Prix at Daytona for the same reasons as the previous season. In 125, the four-cylinder was outmoded and a five-cylinder arrived to take its place during the final Grand Prix in Japan. In 250, the six-cylinder found it difficult to follow the rhythm of the Yamahas and even in 350, Redman was ill treated by a new three-cylinder MV-Agusta : a bad fall during the first Grand Prix, then another in Ulster had almost certainly jeopardised his

Phil Read speeds away to his first title, at the 1964 Tourist Trophy, with the 250 Yamaha RD 56.

The five-cylinder 125, baptised the RC 148, was largely made up of two 50 cc "and a half", and this was without doubt the first really operational five-cylinder in the history of engines. Here Swiss Luigi Taveri is at the controls.

The legendary six-cylinder 250 RC 166, without doubt the most prestigious motorbike in history, is photographed with the team manager of the time, Michihiko Aika (on the right). It is held by one of its veteran mechanics, M. Suzuki.

The twin-cylinder 50 Honda RC 115 produced 13 hp at 20,000 rpm. One must consider that each cylinder had a bore of 34 mm and a four-valve cylinder head. Observe the front brake runner, rather like on a bicycle!

season. Even though, he secured the title, but very narrowly, and a six cylinders was unveiled for the final Grand Prix in Japan.

Suzuki

Disappointing season : Suzuki had made a major effort with a completely new water-cooled twin in 50 cc, but her tuning needed a little longer than foreseen and Anderson could do nothing against the Hondas. He consoled Suzuki by securing the double with Perris in 125, thanks to a new water-cooled twin (unveiled by Degner at the end of the previous season). The 250 scarcely progressed : Perris and Yoshimi Katayama only achieved several isolated results, the machine lacked re-liability and was abandoned halfway through the season. Suzuki however innovated this year by experimenting with an aluminium frame on the 125.

Yamaha

If the 125, from now on water-cooled, remained curiously very discreet (Phil Read walked off with the TT and Mike Duff won at Assen), Read repeated his 250 title and Duff secured the double ahead of Redman's Honda. Concern among the competitors : although their 250 twin was dominating the class, Yamaha launched a four-cylinder V at the penultimate race in Italy.

1966

Honda

The make achieved a unique feat that year : the first five "constructor" titles fell into its hands. Not without ill : offended that the Japanese Grand Prix had been organized at Mount Fuji and not on their own Suzuka circuit, Honda boycotted this final event of the season on the pretext that it was unsafe, and so deprived Taveri of the rider title in 50 cc. Conversely, if Taveri had allowed his teammate Bryans to overtake him in Holland, the latter would have become world champion. Taveri got over it in 125 with the five-cylinder, and the latest recruit in Hailwood dominated the 250 and 350 with the six-cylinder machine. The 500 situation was more delicate, where Honda was the dominant make, but where

Frank Perris and the 125 Suzuki twin at the 1966 Tourist Trophy.

Jim Redman would have become the 500 cc world champion in 1966 with this RC 181. A bad fall at Spa denied him this title.

Hailwood had to leave Agostini and his MV-Agusta to win the rider title by the narrowest margin. Redman, with two wins out of the first two events of the season, was well away, but a heavy fall in the third took him out of the race. Hailwood, called up as the reinforcement, was unable to regain his initial handicap up against Agostini. He consoled himself by winning three races in one day in Czechoslovakia (250, 350, and 500), feat he would repeat several times the following year ! In addition, he also won the ten 250 GPs in which he took part.

Suzuki

Thanks to Honda's withdrawal at Mount Fuji, Anscheidt earned himself the title in 50cc but the 125 twin-cylinder Suzukis were definitely outmoded. Strategically important, the T 500 road model (which would come out the following year) had absorbed a good number of technicians, to the detriment of the development of racing machines.

Yamaha

In 125, a remarkable comeback for the make, whose liquid-cooled twin walked away with half the Grand

Prix : Bill Ivy was threatening Taveri for the title until the very end of the season. With the four-cylinder 250, Read finished regularly on Hailwood's heels and Hasegawa won the final Grand Prix at Mount Fuji… in Honda's absence.

1967

Honda

Honda was taking early retirement : the make knew that the four-stoke was condemned to small capacities, it no longer contested the 50 and 125 cc classes and had stopped all bigger capacity development. Two riders

(Hailwood and Bryans), a team manager (Aika) and six mechanics would suffice for the season. Hailwood snatched the 250 title in style… but only just, having suffered some mechanical breakdowns. He dominated the 350s more easily, but again had to yield in 500 cc, once again by very little to the MV-Agusta of Giacomo Agostini.

Suzuki

In Honda's absence, Anscheidt, Katayama and Stuart Graham not surprisingly offered Suzuki the hat-trick in 50 cc. The twins on the other hand were sliced up in

The entire Honda team was brought back together on the Assen circuit in 1998 to commemorate the fiftieth anniversary of Grand Prix racing. From front to back, the big boss of the racing department during this golden age, Michihiko Aika on a 125 twin, the 250 cc four-cylinder RC 161 of 1960 and RC 162 of 1961, another 125 twin-cylinder RC 125 of 1962 and, at the back, the RC 113 twin-cylinder 50 cc.

125 by the new four-cylinder Yamahas. A four-cylinder put in an appearance at the Japanese Grand Prix (it finished second), but would never again be seen in the World Championship.

Yamaha

A fruitful year in 125, where Bill Ivy's four-cylinder dominated that of his teammate Phil Read, way ahead of the Suzukis. Great struggle in 250, where Read and Ivy did not lose their self respect up against a Hailwood at the peak of his career. In the end, Read even had a bare points lead, but the final classification gave the title to Hailwood who had won five Grand Prix.

Bill Ivy and his four-cylinder 125 Yamaha RA 31A at the start of the 1967 Japanese Grand Prix. In the background, Dave Simmonds' Kawasaki.

With its 42 hp and 136 mph, the four-cylinder 125 RS 67 would without doubt have handsomely rewarded Honda in 1968. But it only put in one Grand Prix appearance at the end of 1967, before Suzuki announced their withdrawal.

Honda

Hailwood and Bryans kept the previous year's machines, but Honda forbade them from entering them in Grand Prix.

Suzuki

Anscheidt was the only one to persevere, without direct factory influence. They dominated in 50cc but with great difficulty up against the still very tender Kreidler, Derbi, and Jamathi single-cylinders, but their twin was logically dominated in 125.

Yamaha

With Honda and Suzuki gone, Read and Ivy dominated the 125 and 250 cc classes without the slightest difficulty. They ought to have shared one title each, but Read, the big head, decided to offer himself both, after having had to swallow the bitterness of the previous year ! Read and Ivy finished the season with equal points and the former only won based on the adding up the times. The regulation had swung the balance in its favor : this tarnished win was the only false note in this ultimate "official" season for the Japanese.

Representing the culmination of a technology were the four-cylinder Yamaha 250 and 125, both world champions in 1968 (as in 1967 for the 125). The 250 RD 05A (above) developed close to 70 hp, while the 125 RA 31 (opposite) just touched 40 hp.

Maturity and dominance

The beginning of the 1960s was a period of euphoria for Japan.
The first highway (Osaka-Nagoya) was officially opened in 1963 and the first Shinkansen (bullet train)
went into operation in 1964 between Tokyo and Osaka.

That year, Tokyo hosted the Olympic Games and great circuits sprouted like weeds : Suzuka (Honda's track) was completed by the end of 1962 ; Ryuyo (that of Suzuki) by the end of 1964 and FISCO (The Fuji International Speedway) in 1966. Yamaha would finish their own track of Fukuroi in 1969 and would open another, at Sugo, in 1973.

Towards a "definite" opening-up

Economically, a profound liberalization took place. For imports, this started off in October 1965. In this field, Japan did not take a great risk: imports of foreign motorbikes that year reached their historic minimum with... seventy-five machines! There would then be a progression, over a five-year period starting in 1967, in the reduction of customs duties by a half, athough they were still at 40 %. Conversely, in 1970 U. S. President Richard Nixon imposed a 10 % tax on Japanese products coming into the United States. Finally, the yen was revalued in 1971, a measure which dominated: the dollar still stood at three hundred and sixty yen (as in 1949 !) and Japanese incomes had again doubled between 1965 and 1970.

The liberalization of capital itself dates from July 1967. With the automobile, this led to mergers (Toyota took over Daihatsu and Hino, Nissan bought up Prince and Fuji). It also led, in 1971, to long-lasting agreements between Mitsubishi and Chrysler and between Isuzu and GM, and later on Mazda and Ford (1979), then Suzuki and GM (1981).

The effects of this measure were less spectacular on the motorbike, but the bankers would profit from letting go of businesses judged non-viable in the long term, and which only political measures had obliged them to support until then.

Economy

Since the end of the nineteenth century, Japanese businesses had been relying on a limited circle of institutional investors more than on a private shareholding. One can find several reasons for this.

In 1966, a man and a woman, Japanese version. Mr. is very proud of his Suzuki B100P (an immense success throughout the world) and certainly plans to take Miss for a ride underneath the flowering cherry trees.

The relatively modest individual living standards, the household habit of choosing a long and securely based savings where personal initiative was lacking in an ultimately considerably collective society (if not collectivist).

It had always been that if savings served in Japan, as elsewhere, to finance businesses, such support should pass via the banks. The subtle difference was in size. The priority of the banks was not to store up important, regulate and secure dividends. Instead, it was to increase their power and that of the businesses they were controlling. They could transfer capital from one branch of activity to another according to requirements. They would also allow themselves to take risks, and to invest in a sector while tolerating short-term losses provided that the market would be profitable in the long-term. They did not have to present a balance sheet every year to watchful shareholders. And they were, evidently, the best placed to predict trends.

We have seen how, in the immediate post-war period, they were more or less under government orders, only obeying commands from on high. The independence of the banks, rediscovered at the end of the 1960s, led to a re-dealing of industrial cards. From now on, investors no longer chose which businesses to support based on purely economical criteria.

The famous MITI would soon have no more than a consultative power, an advisory function. And, paradoxically, the civil service is today even less powerful, the state less heavy, and the government less influential in Japan than in the West.

On the other hand, the big trusts born out of industry at the start of the century (the zaibatsu) had been dismantled post-war to revive and put the keiretsu back on an equal par, like Mitsubishi (whose bank is Honda's major shareholder), Sumimoto (Dunlop, Mazda), Mitsui (Toyota, Yamaha), or immense trading networks like Itochu (godfather of Kawasaki).

Elsewhere in Asia, one comes across this structure for big commercial, industrial, and financial groups (noticeably with the Korean chaebols and the big Indian conglomerates). Their immense ramifications often stretch as far as the political sector and concentrate power and capital by a continually reduced number of directors and shareholders.

Sociology

In 1965, one person in ten owned a car in Tokyo or Osaka. By 1967 this ratio had doubled. The total number of cars went from ten to thirty million private cars

between 1967 and 1976, and for the first time, in 1970, there were more private than commercial vehicles. Nine million driving permits were registered in 1965, but this rose to almost twenty-three million in 1974. Despite this apparent explosion in living standards, the Japanese were not yet used to an easy lifestyle.

Their economy profited from the fact that Westerners in the 1970s, for their part, were fully enjoying a « leisure society », demotivated, almost degenerate, grown soft by the illusion that life was « cool » and that they were owed everything.

But during this period, the Japanese were at work : two thousand three hundred hours per year in 1970. There was a gap between a country turned rich, and its people remaining poor, who were producing motorbikes for a society that to them was still foreign.

Demography

The beginning of the 1960s was also a period of profound industrial change. For Toyota, Taiichi Ohno had invented the "kanban" (tight workflow or just-in-time approach) in 1963. A particularly precious idea in Japan where stocks were as costly as they were bulky and space was at a premium.

As Japanese industry was young and did not burden itself with old-fashioned structures and principles, it unhesitatingly applied these revolutionary manufacturing methods, which traditional western industry would take a long time to understand, let alone to exploit.

Above all, knowing its restrictions and without great island resources, in 1948 Japan adopted a low-birth policy, favoring contraception and authorizing abortion.

Its population, for a long time less than thirty million, had exploded as from the expansionist Meiji era, but had stabilized after the war at around one hundred million.

Industrially, during the boom of this period (and even if the motorbike did not easily lend itself to production-line robotics) this did enable it to automate its manufacture without leaving armies of unemployed out in the cold. The enormous growth in manufacture compensated the gains in productivity.

Westerners, handicapped by the post-war "baby boom", could not even take advantage of this : their workforce having become too abundant in the 1960s, rationalization of the industrial sectors could only be distressing at the human level.

So it was that in 1967 Japan became the second world economic power after the United States.

The scramblers

The first really production scrambler, the 250 Honda CL72, goes back to 1962. A scrambler is in fact a road-bike fitted with raised exhausts, small fuel tank, big handlebars, and studded tires. This type of machine had been developed at the demand of American customers planning to make some off-road trips across the vast desert plains of the United States, with their everyday machine. This idea would soon develop towards even more dual-purpose machines, the "trail bikes", or more professional machines used by farmers.

Do not get taken in by its unflattering appearance: the Honda CT 200 (here in a 1965 version) remained the best-seller in Australia for decades. This worthy representative of the "farmer-bikes", developed from trail bikes for professional use, clearly shows how, in the Antipodes, success sometimes takes very roundabout routes, inconceivable in Europe.

The scrambler formula would in the end develop into, for example, this SL 350 of 1972 with its low-down exhaust. It was however a pure sports machine that even did without an electric starter to stay at 306 lbs. The "trail" formula was not far off.

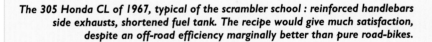

The 305 Honda CL of 1967, typical of the scrambler school : reinforced handlebars side exhausts, shortened fuel tank. The recipe would give much satisfaction, despite an off-road efficiency marginally better than pure road-bikes.

Final purge

Despite all these favorable factors, motorcycle production was dragging its feet beginning in 1963. If there were still around ten manufacturers that year, there were no more than four by 1969 once export figures had definitively gone beyond that of a saturated domestic market. Pigeon and Rabbit, who had placed everything on the home and commercial market, disappeared respectively in 1964 and 1968.

Lilac, like Bridgestone, who were well established across the Atlantic, each gave up before 1970.
Because of a disturbing phenomenon, Japanese output underwent a slight decline in 1967-1968, the first since it had acquired a real industrial status. The reason is clear : the United States, around 1966, had themselves experienced a phase of contraction, following the departure of numerous young men for Vietnam.
Having brought about the birth of the "easy" motorbike

(Yamaha and Suzuki had popularized independent lubrication in 1964), the American approach was no longer the recipe.
Something else had to be invented : this would be, starting in 1970, the ATCs ("All-Terrain Cycles"), then the ATVs ("All-Terrain Vehicles").
In some years, the United States would bring in more of these than of motorbikes up to five hundred thousand units !

The big Japanese makes of the time

Even so, enthusiasts consider the period 1964-1973 as the golden age of the Japanese production motorbike and collectors avidly search out machines from this epoch. One must admit that many models have made their mark at this time. So here they are, assembled in a few pages.

Honda CB 450 : the hi-tech twin

Twin overhead camshaft, valve lift by leaf spring, depression carburetors, Honda had spared no expense in totally eliminating the British motorbike from the American market.

Despite a relatively feeble cubic capacity and a consequent weight (412 lbs.), the CB 450 of 1965 was as powerful (44 hp) and as efficient (125 mph) as the best English 650 cc s, even if its road-holding was somewhat lacking.

No Japanese make proved immediately capable of countering this, except for Kawasaki with their 650 W1 of 1966, a charming old rocker-valve twin developed from the old-style Meguros. Oddly enough, victim of the slowing-down of the American market, the CB 450 would not meet with the success hoped for in the United States. It would, however, establish Honda's reputation in readiness for the CB 750.

The first ATC, named the US90, dates from 1970. We owe this to Honda who, in the first instance, aimed it for leisure ratler than for professional use. There would later be a differentiation between the two activities, and a widespread use of more stable quads.

Suzuki hammers home

Suzuki made a great impact with their 250 T20 of 1965. From one day to the next, this six-speed 29 hp sports model outmoded its Honda rival, the five-speed

The CB 450 was the most advanced and most powerful Japanese machine of its day. Its career would not be on the same leve

At the same time as the 450, Honda was marketing their vertical-cylinder CB 250 and CB 350 with simple OHC, well fleshed out in comparison with the previous CB72/CB77. This version dates from 1970, and its CL scrambler version, in the background, from 1972.

The Monkey and the funpark-motorbikes

The Monkey existed from 1961, as a child's motorbike for recreation parks, but in 1964 Honda developed a public version of it. It was the pioneer of the emerging leisure society ! In all its diverse versions, four hundred and fifty thousand examples of the Monkey alone would be marketed on the other side of the Atlantic.

The Monkey would be followed by many other machines of the same type, like the Dax of 1969 (still made in China), but also Yamaha's Mini Trail (1970), or Suzuki's Van-Van (1971), of which the balloon-tire scooters of the 1980s became the descendants.

The 50 cc Yamaha FT-1 "Mini Trail" of August 1970 resembles in an extremely reduced manner the lines popularized by the 250 DT-1. This machine would have an immense success throughout the world. It had a rotary feed engine.

The Suzuki Van-Van range went from 50 to 125 cc. This Japanese shows just how many accessories were available for it.

Recreational and totally frivolous machine, the 50 Honda Monkey (here in its 1964 version) would often be found on board a boat or at a campsite.

The Honda Dax ST70, in a 1994 version, has remained virtually unchanged since its inception.

24 hp YDS-3. This T20 met with universal market and popularized the idea of a two-stroke which could have both performance and reliability.

The T500, presented in 1967, marks just as important a stage. It was certainly not the first such powerful two-stroke twin : the little make Emuro had launched one in 1960 just before closing down. But this was the first to offer such reliability and such performance : with its 47 horses and its 425 lbs., the T 500 outclassed the 450 Honda for the title of the motorbike with the most power and the best performance on the market, and the Americans became very fond of it. Its racing version, the TR 500, at first air-cooled then liquid-cooled, won two Grand Prix in 1971 and 1973, with Jack Findlay at the controls. The culmination of this big power two-stroke concept would be the three-cylinder GT 750 at the end of 1971.

The first modern mass-produced machine to be equipped with liquid cooling, the big Suzuki would however be eclipsed by the Kawasaki 500s and 750s, more oriented towards pure performance. Their little sisters, the GT 380 and 550 of 1972, with their hybrid capacity, would suffer the same fate, by opting for comfort and touring instead of sport.

It turns out that the 250 Suzuki T20 is even more powerful than the present-day Yamaha, and its six-speed gearbox offers an incomparable whiff of racing.

With the appearance of the T 500 Suzuki in 1967, the two-stroke established itself as a reliable and efficient engine even for big power. Here is the very first 1967 version. From here until its production in 1968, it would receive an oscillating arm extended to over 8 in., so as to improve its stability and to load the front a little during strong acceleration.

Ungainly lines, a drum-brake at the outset of its career (the disc brake for this version would only appear in 1973), a disconcerting engine speed (because of the Ram-Air cylinder block, designed to improve cooling), hybrid cylinders, so many factors in the service of the Suzuki GT, producing 38 hp for 403 lbs. in 380cc (shown here) and 50 hp for 474 lbs. in 550.

At 67 hp for 472 lbs., the GT 750 was well worth a 750 Honda. Appearing belatedly, it would not succeed in establishing the two-stroke in 750. Its drum brake and its insufficient mudguard were frustrating for those wishing to ride at higher speeds. As for the fuchsia color, this was really typical for the period.

No doubt about it: the 250 Yamaha Dt-1 marks a real break with the scramblers. This concerns an off-road bike adapted for the road, and not the opposite. At first, the trail bikes wavered between the front wheels of 19 and 21 inches. The DT-1 developed 19 hp for 247 lbs.

500 Kawasaki H1 racing comes to the street

Yamaha were obviously incapable of doing things like anybody else. Their twin 250 Samurai, in May 1966, had rotary valve (only Bridgestone had dared this arrangement before) and their 500, launched in September 1968, appeared almost revolutionary with its three transversely-mounted cylinders. Olympus, in 1962, had certainly come up with the prototype for such a horizontal three-cylinder at the time, but had not succeeded in marketing it.

Other than its engine, this H1 innovated with condenser discharge electronic ignition, the first on a multi-cylinder road vehicle (the Spanish had already experimented with this technique on off-road monos).

This machine had doubtful road-holding qualities but amazing performance : 60 hp was then the power out-

250 Yamaha DT-1 : the "trail bike" is born

Until then, Yamaha had only produced conventional singles and twins, with more elegance but less performance than the Suzuki equivalents. The DT-1 which came out in March 1968 was therefore an event of first importance. It inaugurated the "trail bike" concept with dual-purpose machine much more for the road than for scrambling. It was in fact a subdued enduro machine, with a geometry really adapted to off-the-road and a civilized engine for daily use. The American market would rave over the DT-1 and its descendants, just as able to stride along the boulevards as to go up and down the desert tracks.

In France, Brigitte Bardot would be the most charming ambassador for the 125 AT-1, the 125 cc version of the DT-1. This machine would even be entitled to an electric starter, to seduce deserters from the automobile. (All rights reserved)

Even for scrambling, Kawasaki stood out from its competitors: the KS 125 of 1974 had rotary valve, like all the little two-stroke singles of this make since 1965, and particularly the 90cc, which would achieve a great and longlasting world success.

The beast in its pure form : the 500 Kawasaki H1 (or Mach III) had a power output fitting for the best racing machines of the day, but its mudguard and its brakes were not really up to it. Paradoxically, this wild, untamed aspect would increase Kawasaki's reputation, symbolized from now on by the unique left-hand exhaust and the twin right-hand pots.

put for a good Grand Prix 500, which propelled its 384 lbs. to 118 mph. With it, Kawasaki would establish his reputation as "rebel" manufacturer, "outside the law", an image that would gain it a faultless loyalty from sporting customers.

As if to back up its commercial career, its competition-customer version, the H1-R, would become 1970 World Champion runner-up with Ginger Molloy behind the untouchable Agostini and his MV-Agusta. Molloy would even win a Grand Prix the following year and Mick Grant would win another in 1975 with a six-speed liquid-cooled "works" version.

It was with their rotary valve twins that Kawasaki built up a reputation for themselves in Europe. Their 250 A1 Samurai and 350 A7 Avenger, strictly identical and here in their 1970 version, were hardly any more powerful than contemporary Yamahas and Suzukis, but they already expressed a separate individuality, even if only from the technological aspect. As was necessary during this period, these models also came in scrambler versions, named SS.

The 500 Kawasaki H1-R, with its 75 hp became the absolute weapon for private entry riders starting in 1969. Unfortunately, its reliability was not perfect, and above all Agostini's official MV-Agusta dominated the debates. The H1-R had to settle for honorary positions.

Honda CB 750 Four : The historic monument

Presented in October 1968, one month after the 500 Kawasaki, this motorbike of 67 hp and 480 lbs. was a total surprise because its development had been jealously guarded.

It is difficult today to imagine the effect that this machine must have when it was launched. The CB 750 cut right across all the other motorbikes of its time and fulfilled the dream of an entire generation of motorcyclists! It was the most efficient and the most prestigious of mass-produced motorbikes in its day, but also, and above all, the symbol of a coming leisure society. The motorbikes of yesterday had been aimed at hardened bikers.

The Honda, itself reliable, clean and almost maintenance-free, appealed to everyone and invented socially acceptable motorcycling. In addition, despite its four-cylinder engine and its front disk brake, which were firsts for the general public of the day, this Honda was less expensive than the 750 three-cylinder Triumph/BSAs.

In short, it was without doubt the most remarkable mass-produced motorbike in history, total fantasy within everybody's pocket, or almost. There is a "before" and

The most beautiful symbol of the end of the 1960s, the Honda CB 750, was the dream of an entire generation. It is presented here in its first K0 version of 1969 (side grill, big logo, finless oil filter and aluminium-coloured calliper).

It would have met with the same success if Honda had conserved the prototype version of 1968 with front drum brake, unveiled here for the first time (left).

an "after" the CB 750, pivotal motorbike par excellence, which would outdate all others. As much for racing, it was equally faultless: with its wins at the "Bol d'Or" 24 hours race in France in September 1969, then at Daytona in March 1970, so launching its career.

This machine would meet with a phenomenal success on all continents. In around ten years Honda would sell one million single OHC four-cylinder models modified from this CB 750, four hundred thousand alone in the United States.

A pity : Kawasaki, who might have been the first to have reinvented the big single cylinder, finally withdrew this carefully designed prototype 500 trail bike in 1973. Yamaha would present their XT 500 at the end of 1975 and Kawasaki would only return with their KL 500 at the Cologne Show in 1982.

The Kawasaki range in 1965. from left to right : At the top, the 125 B8 with double or single saddle and 250 SGT single-cylinder four-stroke. At the bottom, 50 MS Pet, 85 JI, 125 B8T and 650 WI, police type.

In 1971 Honda launched their CB 500, even more refined than the 750. Not particularly racy (48 hp), even a little heavy (406 lbs.), it was on the other hand very luxurious and would seduce the "new motorcyclists". It would encourage Honda to launch a CB 350-four the following year, even more middle-class (34 hp for 375 lbs.).

With its very pared-down lines, its "4-in-1" exhaust, its overtly sober decoration, the CB 400 Four of 1977 would mark Honda's return to more racy four-cylinder machines.

Suzuki T 90/T 125 : Suzuki's daring creations

Suzuki was the make for both the conformists…and the audacious. Its T 90 (T 125 in Europe), appearing in 1969, is witness to this. With its horizontal cylinders, its raised exhausts like scramblers, its very tapered fuel tank, its absence of side covers and its pancake headlamp, this machine tried to revive the 125 sporting twin type. It proved a bitter setback and Suzuki would have to return to a more conventional formula. Collectors, on the other hand, are today very fond of this strange model.

650 Yamaha XS-1: The modern twin, half-English, half-Japanese

Appearing one year after the CB 750 and three years after the 650 Kawasaki W1, the Yamaha XS-1 might seem insignificant. It was however a noteworthy event in that this was Yamaha's first four-stroke motorbike. The engineering emerged from an old Hosk project, tastefully brought up to date through a collaboration between Yamaha and Toyota on the 2000 GT project. If it resumed the English-style twin format, the XS-1 also received a boxed cylinder block, vacuum carbs, and an overhead camshaft.

Neither the engine, nor the frame were exceptional, but the XS-1 knew how to build up a strong image which would ensure a long and happy career. In addition, the

Called the Wolf in 90cc, or Flying Leopard in 125, this Suzuki cut right across all the motorbikes of the day. It would not meet with much esteem, even when its exhaust took on a more classic form (lower down).

To only see in the 650 XS-1 a pale copy of an English twin would be to fall victim to an optical illusion. As a matter of fact, this machine attempted to bring back their look, but its technology was perfectly up-to-date.

Metallurgy (cylinder treatments), airtightness (crankshaft joints, piston circles), scavenging (intakes, transfers, exhausts), electronic ignition: never in history had a type of engine progressed so quickly. The development would continue into the 1980s with important work on variable geometry exhausts (section, volume or diagram).

Kawasaki 350 S2 and 750 H2 : The maturity of a school

If the 500 H1 had blown people's minds with its staggering performances, the S2 and H2 launched at the end of 1971 would make an equivalent mark on their epoch, with their power output (45 hp for the 350, 74 hp for the 750) and with their lines.

In racing, both of them enjoyed a fine career. The "little one" would earn its reputation in one of the first really promotional racing formula, the famous Kawasaki Cup which discovered numerous young talents, like Patrick Pons. As for the "big one", in a race version called the H2-R, it could be considered as the "moral" champion of Europe in the 1976 750 cc. season, despite ferocious competition from the Yamaha TZ 750s.

These two models also innovated in the field of style, in considerably resorting to plastics (in particular the front mudguard) and above all in the adoption of a leather seat cowl (also in plastic) which would subsequently be found a great deal elsewhere. With two right-hand exhausts, one left-hand, and a rear raised up like a chicken's bum, the "three-legged Kawa" could be recognized at a

XS-1 would open up the way to an entire generation of far more innovative Yamaha four-stroke twins.

350 Yamaha R5: The triumph of design

In the genealogy of Yamaha two-stoke twins, the 350 R of 1970 cosmetically occupies a place apart. With its extremely elegant and sculptured lines, it is even the symbol of the ultimate design, with its engine housing painted black, its daring colours (purple or mustard yellow) at a period when red or blue were the norm, and the care given the design of the smallest parts.

Those who prefer engineering to aesthetics, will recall from this period Yamaha's contribution to two-stroke progress, with the general use of poppet valves starting in 1971. This technology would be the crowning achievement of the enormous effort put in by Yamaha (and Suzuki) on the two-stroke over fifteen years, improving performance, reliability, and consumption.

Without doubt one of the prettiest motorbikes in its day, the 350 Yamaha R5 (and its 250 version the DS 7) had been given an extreme attention to detail : mudguards, fork joints, chain cowling, exhaust curvature, cylinders, cylinder heads and, of course, tank, side caches and engine cowls : this machine had clearly been "designed".

The 750 H2 (or Mach IV) resumed the lines of the 350 S2, but its exhausts swept back more conventionally. This machine would for a long time be the authority in pure performance, but its fuel consumption, totally abnormal compared with that of the 500 H1,could go beyond the 15 liters/100 km !

considerable distance, daily building up the legend of a "clan" knit together by real buffs. Sign of the times, the real sportsmen who used the three-cylinder Kawasakis did not have the right to electric starting.

The 350 S2 was one of the most innovative machines in terms of construction materials: front mudguard in plastic and stepped seat would become the trend. Even more becoming manner its 250 S1 version would come in white, with a most pleasing effect of green lines. Eventually this 350 would turn into a less original 400 S3.

Yamaha GL 750 :
The pretty dream

Amazement in October 1971 : Yamaha presented a superb machine, decked out in beautifully glittering paintwork, a white saddle and above all an incredible four-cylinders in-line, two-stroke, water-cooled with fuel injection. This fabulous machine would not have any commercial follow-up. To console its fans, the 1973 Grand Prix 500 then the 1974 TZ 750 would take up its engine design (without injection) and give it one of the finest sporting careers as one might imagine.

Everything is beautiful in the lines of the 250 XL : its brakes, its mudguard, its tank, its exhaust right up to the carburetor. At 22 hp for 280 lbs., this was, moreover an efficient and powerful machine.

This show prototype caused a great deal of spilled ink and considerable saliva between 1971 and 1972. Even if they were unable to find it at their dealer's, its admirers could cheer on its racing version in 500 Grand Prix.

In Japan, the 900 Kawasaki Z1 existed in 750cc as the Z2. The two machines were strictly identical externally, except for the rear tire.

Honda XL 250 : Little single will become big

Introduced in April 1972, the XL 250 was not only the first four-stroke trail bike; it was also the first large production "four-valve". This technical approach would only come to be followed in April 1973 by the TX 500 Yamaha. With its very elegant lines but also its good performance (the weight was kept within reasonable limits due to the use of magnesium for the side motor-housings), the XL opened up the way for modern trail bikes.

900 Kawasaki Z1 : The same, but better

At Kawasaki, they had always been ready to listen to the American market, about which they had prematurely guessed that it was ripe for a powerful multi-cylinder machine.

By 1968, the project was very advanced…when Honda launched their own CB 750. The two machines were so close that, so as not to appear copycats, Kawasaki continued to modify their copy for another four years. Appearing in the summer of 1972, the 900 Z1 was a Honda… but better : twin overhead camshafts, better road-holding, better braking, better performance (it was, with its 82 hp and its 507 lbs., the most powerful motorbike on the market), better mechanical accessibi-

lity, better reliability (reinforced chain) and taking account of future anti-pollution regulations.

This was the least they could do after a delay of four years, but it was one hell of a performance : Kawasaki were then producing six times fewer motorbikes than Honda and neither Yamaha nor Suzuki had, in the meantime, been capable of delivering the slightest coherent response to the devilish CB 750.

If the three-cylinder two-strokes had established Kawasaki's sporting reputation, the Z1 hallmarked their reputation for seriousness.

Other priorities

In January 1968 Honda and Suzuki, then Yamaha at the end of 1968, successively announced their withdrawal from Grand Prix racing. The reason for this decision was not uniquely technical. Of course, the International Motorcycling Federation, considering race budgets had become excessive, issued a new regulation that rendered obsolete even the most sophisticated Japanese machines and was meant to give an opportunity back to the small European manufacturers. As of 1969, the 50cc would be limited to a single cylinder and the 125 cc would not be able to use more than two. As of 1970, the 250s would have limits of two cylinders, with four cylinders for the 350 and 500, and all of them would be limited to six-speed gearshifts, but no more.

The 250 Yamaha TD-2 (and its 350 version, the TR-2) would be one of the most titled competition-production bikes in history. Its race wins would be without equal, despite a really ordinary basic technology taken from the 250 DS-6 of 1968, with its vertically mounted cowling.

For the manufacturers, this was a good excuse. In fact, while racing at first served to promote their image, had fulfilled its role. Honda, by snatching all the solo titles in 1966 (50, 125, 250, 350, and 500 cc) had achieved a feat without precedent. But he also guessed that their four-strokes would not be able to resist the progress of the two strokes for long. Between 1961 and 1968, the Japanese three had just won thirty world Grand Prix titles. Their reputation and their prestige was by now immense, so they could move on to other things, and in particular to their industrial consolidation, with the automobile in mind.

This massive Grand Prix presence had been financially ruinous. In 1964, Honda had sent nineteen machines to the Tourist Trophy, and it was still not yet contesting the 500 class. At the same event the following year, Suzuki (only entered for three classes) dispatched seventeen motorbikes and twenty mechanics. It is from this period that the tradition dates of either destroying the machines at the end of the season or of making gifts of them to the riders: in this way the costs of repatriation and of storage were reduced.

And yet this enormous investment did not prevent Honda, between 1965 and 1966, from losing out on 30% of their exports to the United States (unimpressed by the European Grand Prix). Suzuki was also trying to get their breath back : through their excessive loyalty to the two-stroke, their world sales made no headway between 1967 and 1970. And more than this, one or the other were from now on very involved with the automobile and the motorbike had to take second place.

Not completely absent

This withdrawal did not mean that Grand Prix returned to European territory. In 125, a Kawasaki won the 1969 title with Dave Simmonds. Anscheidt's old Suzuki took it over in 1970 in the hands of Dieter Braun, and Graham's would still be world champion runner-up in 1971 with Barry Sheene.

Practically unchanged, this engineering would still be competitive ten years after its first appearance, sometimes under borrowed names (Malanca, for example, for the Suzuki), because the unbridled competition between the Japanese had raised performance to a level inconceivable at the beginning of the 1960s. The forty-two horsepower of a 125 Suzuki, the seventy horsepower of a 250 Yamaha 4, would only be reached a decade later. In the meantime, the 250s became the exclusive domain of the 44hp Yamaha TD-2 "private racing" machines, often supported (discreetly) by the factory. In reality, even without specifically supplying "official" machines, Yahama would be the only one out of the Big Four never to abandon the Grand Prix world from 1963 until today… So it was that in 1970, through the intermediary of their European subsidiary, Rod Gould was backed in his conquest of the 250 title. This support continued up to 1975 for Kent Andersson's 125, via a Scandinavian importer, as well as a great many 250s between 1971 and 1973.

Only the lone marksman Phil Read managed to win the 250 title in 1971 without any factory support, but simply by entrusting his preparation to the German Helmut Fath.

The others go away, Kawasaki arrives

As usual, Kawasaki were going in the opposite direction to their three competitors. It was just as they were thinking of turning away from Grand Prix at the end of 1965 that they entered the Japan Grand Prix. Their 1966 season was ruined by Toshio Fujii's fatal fall during trials at the Isle of Man TT, and the factory would only re-appear at the final event, in Japan. Araoka finished seventh, Simmonds eighth, and Chris Vincent (who replaced Degner, injured during the trials) tenth. This was also the occasion to unveil a four-cylinder that only put in a brief appearance.

In 1967, Dave Simmonds campaigned for an entire season but the factory only gave him limited support. Despite the absence of the five-cylinder Hondas, his twin was limited against the Yamaha 4s and even again the more seasoned Suzuki twins. Once again, only the final Japan Grand Prix let them correct the balance: the Kawasakis finished third and fourth in the hands of Kanaya and Morishita. In 1968, Kawasaki had still not entered their four-cylinder: the firm had halted its development after the FIM had announced the limitation on the number of cylinders for the coming season. And Simmonds, physically weak following a serious fall at the end of the previous season, did not obtain any good results. He would catch up the following year with,

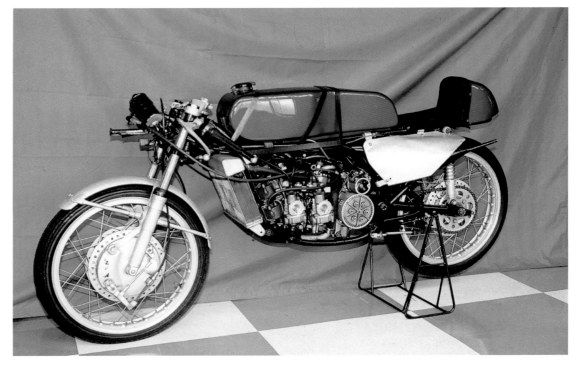

The 125 Kawasaki KR3 (or KA-2) would only be seen once in Grand Prix, in 1966. Its engine had twin crankshafts, one behind the other, like the 250 Suzuki but unlike the 125 Suzuki and the Yamahas. On the other hand, the cylinders were slightly opened out, in a V, to allow quadruple exhausts which had been directed upwards, to pass in front.

As 1969 World champion, the 125 KR2 (or KA-1) returned to a fairly traditional configuration, identical to those of Yamaha and Suzuki in the years before.

itself by choosing the race classes neglected by their competitors. The machine was a modified version of the 125 B8 from the previous year, one of the very first complete motorbikes to carry the Kawasaki name. It was worth the effort : the machine bagged the six first places in the Japanese championship in its class !

The make would only win its first title in 1995, with Stefan Everts in 250, immediately followed the year after by that of the Frenchman Tortelli in 125! Until then, Kawasaki had above all invested in the American championship, which the make would win in 1972, with Brad Lackey.

In Grand Prix, it was to Suzuki that one credits the first attempt at the World Championship, starting in 1965, and the 250 title came in 1970 with Joël Robert. For Suzuki this would be the first in a formidable run of victories, which would in particular include ten consecutive 125 titles (from 1975 to 1984). The "yellow make" is today the most crowned in moto-cross, with twenty-seven world titles by the end of 1999.

Yamaha followed suit in 1972 and clinched their first 250 title in 1973, with Hakan Andersson and a technology which quickly gained a following. The rear suspension of his machine had a single combined spring buffer, horizontally positioned under the fuel tank and activated by triangulate cantilever swing arm. By the important clearance that this gave, by the production quality of its shock absorbers, by the sturdiness it gave to the swing arm, this configuration gave excellent re-

very simply, the world title. It had been Yamaha's turn to leave, limiting competition to a few European singles as well as the old Suzuki twins of Braun and Dongen. Without any support from the factory and despite a harsh lack of spare parts, Simmonds finished by making an impact. He even finished fourth in the 1970 Championship.

Moto-cross,
above all a Suzuki affair

Curiously, the first of the present-day big manufacturers to take an interest in motocross was Kawasaki. In fact, starting in 1963 there was a 125 from this make at the championship of Japan, which drew attention to

With the backdrop of Mount Fuji, a motocross event in the early 1960s. The machine is a little Honda horizontal single.

One of the first "official" Suzuki moto-cross bikes, this 250 RH 67 of 1967 was not yet ready for a world title.

In 1970, the Belgian Joël Robert was the first Japanese works rider to become world moto-cross champion, with this 250 Suzuki.

In 1975 Suzuki entered this RA in the 125 cc Grand Prix. It would win the first world title awarded for this capacity, thanks to the Belgian Gaston Rahier.

A fruitful year in 1975 for the Belgian Roger de Coster, who again won the 500 cc title at the controls of his Suzuki RN.

Harry Everts and his 125 Suzuki in 1980, en route to the second of his three consecutive world titles in this class.

sults in traction. It would be fitted to a great many mass-produced Yamahas starting the next year.

Honda themselves only returned to Grand Prix racing in 1975 to win their first 500 title in 1979 with Graham Noyce. Meanwhile, the world leader would be involved in the American championship which at the time counted for more in marketing terms than the world championship.

Where customers were concerned, the Big Four had began to sell moto-cross machines in 1972, with the exception once again of Kawasaki which had been going since 1963 with their B 8M !

It was the quality of its suspension system that enabled the 250 Yamaha to widen the gap between itself and its pursuers in the 250 World Championship of 1973.

Number One

In March 1970, Dick Mann's Honda CR 750 put an end to an era by winning the Daytona 200, the most prestigious speed event contested in America. Until then, only British or American manufacturers had held this title: Suzuki had only just failed with a second place the year before, with Ron Grant and the TR 500. From now on, and after the intermediate Triumph-BSA in 1971, this race would become the preserve of the Japanese and more precisely of Yamaha, who would win thirteen straight titles from 1972 to 1984. Unwritten protectionist rules made clear that, since the war, never had the US championship been won by

other than an American or a British machine. In 1973, Kenny Roberts snatched this title away at the handlebars of his Yamahas, two-stroke singles and a twin based on the 650 XS-1. He would repeat the achievement the following year after having tantalized

Called YZ 624, here is the first real moto-cross Yamaha, a 250 entered for Mount Asama in 1970 and still equipped with a conventional rear suspension.

the Europeans on their home ground. The symbol escaped no-one : if European Grand Prix were no longer important, the image in the United States was becoming of primary importance.

The rebirth of the Bol d'Or

In 1969, France revived as its only internationally prestigious event, interrupted since 1960, was reborn. The Bol d'Or twenty-four-hour race, was put back on its feet at Montlhéry, and the Honda CR 750 of Michel Rougerie and Daniel Urdich won it ahead of three Kawasaki H1 500s : Japan was already making its mark for the coming 1970s.

In 1970 and 1971, the Triumph-BSAs had the advantage but, starting the following year, it was the Paris dealer Japauto who came up trumps with a Honda boosted to 696 cc.

He would win twice in succession, with Debrocq and Ruiz in 1972 then Debrocq and Tchernine in 1973. From then on, the Bol d'Or would no longer elude the Japanese manufacturers.

Michel Rougerie and Daniel Urdich won the first Bol d'Or at its revival in 1969 and six months later Dick Mann would win the Daytona 200 on a similar machine. What better way to launch the commercial career of the CB 750, as if it really needed it.

Thierry Tchernine and the 1000 Japauto, victorious at the 1973 Bol d'Or. The streamlining of this machine was not lacking in originality and Japauto did not hesitate to market it in kit form, increasing the 750 Hondas to 969 cc.

THE INDUSTRY FROM 1973 TO 1978

From the USA to Europe

In 1973, the American market was still vital since it represented more than one million five hundred thousand units per year. The first oil crisis, that year, caused its dramatic fall and it passed below the million mark by 1978.

The crisis finished off the British industry, very dependant on the American market, and caused two reactions from the Japanese manufacturers:

Firstly the conception of more "civil" motorbikes, better behaved, to satisfy a new American mentality. Towards this tendency came a concerted contribution by Yamaha and Kawasaki to the four-stroke, Suzuki trying to sell two-strokes which nobody wanted any more.

Next, and subsequently, the refocusing on Europe. As the first approach was not enough to re-launch sales, those who were heavily involved would adjust their sights starting in 1976 and would conceive more sporting machines, particularly suited to European taste.

Given that the target was now the United States, of the Big Four, Kawasaki would be the most involved in engine de-tuning, be it with the KZ 400 of 1974 or this KZ 750 of 1976. A point in common for these two sanitised twin-cylinder four-strokes (as also with the Yamaha TX): a con-rod assembly inclined by 360° but with force balance beams. The 750 was entitled, as a bonus, to a twin overhead camshaft.

Kawasaki quickly understood they had taken the wrong direction with their "over-American" KZ twins. So their twin overhead camshaft quad, the Z 650 of 1977 had modern engineering, performance, and brilliantly restored the racing image of the make, with its 64 hp for 465 lbs. Aesthetically, it still remained close to the previously mentioned "sanitized" twin.

Even presented by Jarno Saarinen, the super-champion at the start of the 1970s, the TX 750 Yamaha launched in 1972 would be given a cool reception. Its engine did, however, represent a substantial effort by the make, but with 63 hp for 463 lbs, there was nothing exciting about it and its reputation for fragility would not exactly help it either.

Fuel crisis and pollution

Productivity slowed in 1975-1976 because the home market was permanently stagnating, if only because of the new and tougher driving licence for over 400 cc. Japan also depended on the Middle East for 80 % of its fuel supply, and the coast of petroleum increased by 217 % while inflation in Japan amounted to 24.5 % in 1974. This was a record for an industrialized country and contributed to the first decline in the gross national product since the war. Japanese cars, in general small and not very thirsty, were somewhat favored, but the motorbike suffered.

It also suffered for another reason : new norms for nitrogen oxide (NO x) rates in exhaust emissions would come into force in Japan as of 1978. These strict norms would only be adopted by the United States in 1983. The manufacturers, to meet with this, encountered huge difficulties that resulted, for the automobile, in the adoption of electronic fuel injection and the catalytic converter. In 1975, 36 % of research and development costs were devoted to the reduction of exhaust emissions and the brainpower put onto this task was borrowed from the racing department.

New issues

That explains Yamaha's and Suzuki's withdrawal from racing in 1976 (in fact, they would stay in there, but with outside support) during a globally troubled period. There was a reshuffle for the direction of the world's top manufacturer. S. Honda and T. Fujisawa retired and were replaced by K. Kawashima at the end of 1973. This was also the case at Yamaha, where H. Koike became executive chairman in 1974. As for Suzuki, whose two-strokes were less and less respected in both the United States and in Japan, he studied all the alternative routes, like the Wankel engine.

Confident in their recovery, Kawasaki built a factory in the United States in 1974. Despite appearances, Kawasaki's choice proved sound. This is because the slowdown observed around 1975 was as much due to the fuel crisis as the 10% devaluation of the dollar.

The Yamaha XS 750 of 1976 did not lack in originality with its shaft transmission and three-cylinder powerplant. As for the TX 750, the design office at Porsche had been consulted for the assembly of this technology, then new to Yamaha. The XS 750 would also innovate with its branch wheels.

Honda and Kawasaki both experimented with the technology of the Wankel engine around 1970, but neither one nor the other ventured into production. These two prototypes were not even unveiled at the time, unlike that of Yamaha.

The Wankel's dead end

At the start of the 1970s, for a manufacturer like Suzuki to go from the two-stroke to the Wankel engine, which featured similar technology, seemed more logical than going from two-stroke to four-stroke. This type of engine was very promising and the other Big Three also tested it out during that period. Yamaha even seriously envisaged its production with the RZ 201 prototype presented at the end of 1972. But in the end, only Suzuki went ahead with their RE-5 in the autumn of 1973. Sadly, its disturbing appearance (due, it seems, to the Italian automobile designer Giugaro who was then trying out the motorbike styling) and its mediocre performance, coupled to the absence in vibration (and in character) of its engineering would put off the clientele, despite a spectacular American launch in the presence of the astronaut Neil Armstrong. The Wankel, whose potential was very real, would be banished because of its fuel consumption and the difficulties encountered by car makers in meeting emissions' standards. For their part, Suzuki would pour a great deal of money into this project, and for this reason would lag well behind the others...like going over to four-strokes !

The Suzuki RE-5 (christened RX-5 at the time of its launch) was a bitter setback that cost Suzuki dearly. Heavy, not very efficient (62 hp for 507 lbs.), aesthetically too original (even if only in its instrument panel or its rear lamp), not really reliable and ill-served by an excessive fuel consumption, it could scarcely hope for real success except with collectors.

The RZ 201, presented at the end of 1971, might have been a retort to the Suzuki RE-5. Fortunately, Yamaha decided not to put it into production. At any rate, its appearance was less disturbing than its rival's, and its engine was better developed because it included two rotors and side intake (the Suzuki settled for a single rotor and peripheral intake).

The 1000 Gold Wing looked like no other existing motorbike. Above all it brought a comfort, a softness, and a refinement unknown until then. Despite its weight (571 lbs. for 80 hp) and a sophistication that, at the time, appeared excessive, it would enjoy a remarkable career, still going strong, especially in America today.

Honda Gold Wing :
When the cat is no longer there...

Soichiro Honda had only sworn by the four-stroke and air-cooling. With Hondas' retirement in September 1973, K. Kawashima had complete freedom to launch projects cutting right cross the company's original lines. Since 1973, the firm was therefore producing moto-cross and enduro two-strokes (developed in the patron's ignorance !) and launched the GL 1000 Gold Wing at the end of 1974. This motorcycle would make its mark. Considering its manufacturer, it had a daring technology : its water-cooled, flat four cylinders, below-saddle fuel tank, rear disc brake, even its shaft transmission were all important innovations. For its time, it had the sought-after clean and civil aspect. For America, it embodied excess and affluence. For Japan, it resumed impeccable finish and faultless fitting-out. And finally for Europe, it combined the open road advantages of the BMWs. Not therefore astonishing that this machine met with phenomenal success for over twenty years on every continent.

In 1988, having evolved as a 1,100 then 1,200 cc, the GoldWing took one further step up to a flat six-cylinder 1,500 cc... Even heavier, even more luxurious, it would from then on be crowned as the Queen of the open roadsters. One technological originality of the machine : an electric reverse gear for on-foot manoeuvring.

Perfect symbol and culmination of Honda's over cautious development at the start of the 1970s : the 750 automatic of 1976. Like the 400 automatic developed on the basis of the 400 T, the CB 750 AT in fact had a two-speed gearbox (short and long). But with a torque converter, the absence of a clutch enabled the rider to start up with either one.

The CB 250 and 400 T of 1977 not only innovated with their rounded-off lines. Their new engine with three valves per cylinder and con-road assembly turned at 360° gave them a temperament just right for the seduction of European users.

Direct on-site manufacture was one useful way of cushioning currency fluctuations. Honda, normally the pioneer, would not follow Kawasaki to the United States until 1979 : they had already been installed in Mexico since 1971 and in Brazil since 1977. But there was one unmistakable sign from this manufacturer : in 1976, the sales figures for their automotive division were higher than the motorbike sector. And from then on this gap would not stop widening.

From the Honda "civics" to the comeback

The manufacturer whose about-turn during the 1970s would be the most spectacular was Honda. Beginning in 1973, the firm was clearly "slipping" towards "soft" motorbikes, and even finished by downgrading their successful models like the XL 250, the CB 450, or the CB 750, which had been dangerously putting on weight in 1974-75. The height of bad taste was reached with the automatic version of the historic 750, in 1976, which developed no more than forty-seven horsepower : in other words twenty less than the original version ! Honda however quickly understood their mistake and, through the dynamism of the engineer Shoichiro Irimajiri, from who came the majority of Grand Prix

machines of the 1960s, entirely renewed their line-up. They started in 1977 with a 750 that fully regained its health (the F2). With nearly all the medium-powered machines re-endowed with seduction and performance, Honda made a quick and successful comeback.
It was about time, because its market position had suffered a spectacular downfall in just three years. The moral of the story is that dedicated motorcyclists

This 1973 MT 250 Elsinore was the first emancipation attempt by Honda from their founder : in other words, the first two-stroke for the make in twenty years. The engine base of this trial-bike would also be used in motocross.

throughout the world remained rebels, for whom "reasonable" arguments had absolutely no impact.

Honda hammers home

To really confirm that it counted on regaining its place as leader as quickly as possible, Honda went even further, at the end of 1977, with two spectacular models that, in different ways, would make their mark on the time. Both came from S. Irimajiri, who certainly made sure of his role as major craftsman in this return to the top.
The CX 500 was surprising in more ways than one. At first it was… ugly. Then it was… excellent : it was the best average-powered roadster of its epoch. Comfortable and powerful, it would delight generations of regular bikers little attracted to big multicylinder machines. Technically, it wasn't lacking in originality, with its water-cooled 80° V-twin, its four rocker-arm, cylinder blocks that had been pivoted to make space at knee-level and its composite wheel spokes. For Honda, the CX would initiate a long tradition of average-powered V-twins, well suited to open touring. Technically less original, its heirs, the VT 500 in 1983 then the NTV 650 of 1988, would also shine by their efficiency rather than by their

Voluminous for a 500, but also very powerful (48 hp for 480 lbs.), despite its rocker valve and its touring use, the CX 500 would make a mark on its time while lending itself as much to long-distance, heavily loaded trips as to racing.

looks… almost as if, in this market niche, beauty might appear suspect !

The CBX 1000 was intended to bring back the image of Hailwood's 250s and 350s. Its chassis returned to the principle of a backbone under which the engine was hung. And the engine was an impressive transversely-mounted six-cylinders in-line, as on the Benelli Sei marketed since 1974. Simply, the Honda also counted two overhead camshafts, four valves per cylinder and six carburetors. In short, a real racing engine. Posting a trifling 105 hp, the CBX was the first mass-produced motorcycle to go beyond the 100 hp mark. It was also the first motorcycle (together with the CX) to adopt tubeless tires. Several scooters had already experimented with this technology in the 1960s, but until then no motorbike.

In fact, too heavy (544 lbs.), too bulky, and too complex, the CBX was not the sports model everybody had been dreaming about. Not that it mattered as this role would be well reserved for the 900 Bol d'Or, less powerful but more compact. The CBX would retain the prestige and the image of a totally novel and noble engineering approach that has still not been outmoded.

Europe becomes a priority

In reality, all the manufacturers had grasped the need for compensating for the decline in the American market by giving more importance to a European market very fond of both technology and of sport. In both these aspects the European biker would be spoiled.It was Yamaha who first took care of this in 1976, with two key models, whose commercial success would be well contrasted.

The XS 500 was the successor of the TX 500 of 1973, but innovated with its solid-spoke wheels, front and rear disc brakes, and above all by its unassuming looks, with angular lines and matte paintwork. Handicapped by doubtful reliability due to its balance arms system, the XS 500 would not harvest the fruits of its boldness, but it would at least make a mark on its time.

In contrast to the very sophisticated XS 500, the totally simple XT 500 with twin valves and simple camshaft, was the true concept of the "big single", a basic, even stark motorbike, dressed up as a trail-bike. Nobody believed it, Yamaha did it, and from this machine with its strong personality, the firm gained an immense reputation among lovers of "real" motorbikes. Everyone greeted the return to true values, to vibrations, to starting difficulties, in short, to motorbikes of character. And consecutive wins in the first two Paris-Dakar race, in 1979 and 1980 would establish the legend. It was again Suzuki, whose four-cylinder four-stroke GS 750 marketed in 1977 persuaded people to forget about all its mistakes from the beginning of the decade. To catch up on lost time, Suzuki was frankly inspired, without saying anything more, by the four-stroke Kawasakis. This would result in something of a quarrel between the two makes, but the result was : fantastic ! Aesthetically sensible, as powerful as reliable, this ma-

In its configuration, the CBX 1000 is reminiscent of Hailwood's fabulous 250. In reality, its weight did not really make it into a racing bike, but its prestige remains without equal even today.

In 1978, Honda launched their N series whose name, Eurostyle, was a giveaway : from now on this was about winning back a sporting public, after twenty years of making the United states a priority.

You had to be bold to launch a machine like this in 1976 ! The XS 500 Yamaha astonished more by its sharp angles, solid-spoke wheels and its matte paintwork than by its engine, one of the first mass-production, "four valves-twin shaft" types.

chine would reconcile the public with the make and put Suzuki back on the rails after the serious strategic error of the Wankel. With the GS 750, the make was fully aware of risking everything, double or nothing, and for this Suzuki had chosen the most costly and the most sophisticated technology, particularly in metallurgy, in order to make the best 750 of the time. A successful wager : with its sisters, the GS400 and 550, this first four-stroke was a master stroke.

It was in the end Honda who, in 1978, unambiguously launched their "Eurostyle" line. The engineer S. Irimajiri did not hide it : he wanted to re-establish Honda for top class performance. The 250 and 400 "N"s were directly developed from the "T" twins of 1977, but with sharp edges which made their line less tubby, more aggressive. As for the Bol d'Or, its name alone summed it all up : this CB 900F of 95 hp for

Here is the return to rugged, virile motorcycles that vibrated, with the Yamaha XT 500 of February 1976. Yamaha had understood that the "macho" that slumbers in every motorcyclist only needed waking up. In this first version, the exhaust passed even lower, but it would soon be lifted up in a more off-road style. Pure performance was modest (30 hp, 306 lbs., 87 mph), but with a really toughened-up character.

Even though looking a little humdrum, the GS 750 presented at the end of 1976 was Suzuki's first four-stroke in twenty years and a complete success. One must say that the make had no room left for mistakes after their great failure with the rotary engine. With its 68 hp for 491 lbs., the GS offered a rare consistency. It would be marketed in Europe equipped with a front twin disc.

A single name shows how Honda changed policy in 1978. This CB 900 F will be known better as the "Bol d'Or" and the manufacturer will try to get the most out of its victories in endurance racing.

514 lb. was meant to be the queen of the sports models, and the titles gathered in by Honda since 1976 in the endurance championship of Europe supported its commercial success.

The "superbikes" era

With its CBX, Honda had set off hostilities. By the end of 1977, the other manufacturers threw themselves one by-one-into the race for pure performance : it was a formula as old as the motorbike, but still remains a formula on both sides of the Atlantic or the Pacific. The answers from Suzuki and Kawasaki were timid : the former proposed a more powerful GS 1000 although less homogenous than the 750, the latter pre-

Jean-Claude Olivier, the Yamaha importer for France, showed off just what an XS 1100 could do during the launch of this model in the neighbourhood of Dakar at the end of 1977.

sented a Z1-R whose principle merit was to be the first Japanese machine to be given (small) mass-produced streamlining.

Yamaha's riposte was more impressive. The XS 1100, the first four-cylinder four-stroke for the make, was not only powerful (95 hp), it also innovated stylistically (with its rectangular headlamp, in particular). Above all it defined itself in a way that ensured it a place apart in the "big" concert of the time : its Hotchkiss drive and its sizeable tank enabled it to seduce both the hardened biker as well as the sportsrider.

How else to swell the pride of a manufacturer like Yamaha for whom, really, everything was successful during this period.

Yamaha plays with low power (as well)

In 1977, in fact, while Honda was monopolizing attention with one spectacular model after another, Yamaha (as well) was thinking about efficiency and gross sales. Two symbols bear witness to this.

Their Passol scooter marks a return to the scooter, after the unfortunate attempt with the SC-1 in 1960. Although the scooter was considered quaintb and out of fashion, Yamaha redirected it towards the gentler sex. Bright colors, featherweight (100 lbs.), and sold at a very easy price, the Passol would very quickly become

Daihatsu, the last of its kind

In 1978, Daihatsu, the last of the "small" manufacturers stopped its production of motorcycles. In fact, only two models had remained in its catalogue until then and were somewhat different from the rest of the motorcycles made in Japan : an articulated three wheeler of 50 cc named Hallo and the Solex 5000 imported as is from France. Actually, Daihatsu's return to motorcycling was recent when it decided to stop such activity as the company was already heavily involved in automobile manufacturing. In 1974, the Hallo came too early on the market as proven by the success, a few years later, of the Honda Stream and Gyro. In addition, the Solex was simply too small and too fragile to survive in the modern Japanese urban environment.

Today, Daihatsu is a satellite of Toyota.

Inspired from the British Ariel 3 of 1970, the 50 Daihatsu Hallo of 1974 combined the stability of a three wheeler and the bending of a motorcycle in curves. This concept was simply too new to catch on when it was released. Honda did better by waiting until 1980 to launch its Stream model.

The 1000 Kawasaki Z1-R was certainly the first streamlined Japanese production bike to be distributed, but its tank had a ridiculously small capacity and did not permit any extensive trips, while its road-holding was slack.

the faithful pilot of a powerful return to favor of the scooter in Japan and then throughout the whole world.

As for the DT 125 MX, a simple figure will illustrate its importance : more than one hundred thousand examples would be distributed in France alone, something that no other motorbike had ever or has since achieved. The trump cards of the DT-MX ? Performance, reliability, irresistible lines and Yamaha's strong reputation with trail-bikes : the DT-MX combined the image of the XT 500 (with its wins in African rallying) with the moto-cross YZ (World Champion in 1973, 1977, and 1978).

The DT 125 MX would achieve an unprecedented success: this remarkable little machine, reasonable and efficient, safe and amusing, would quickly become the most distributed motorbike on the French market.

Each one returns on its own way

Honda and Suzuki had left the Grand Prix scene at the start of 1968. Kawasaki had never been seriously involved but had made its presence felt between 1967 and 1970. Yamaha, for its part, had officially withdrawn at the end of 1968, but had also returned through the more discreet go-between of its importers and very competitive private racing machines in 125, 250, 350 and even 750 cc (starting in 1974).

With perfect logic, the Finn Jarno Saarinen ought to have become the first 500 world champion on a Japanese machine. Fate would decide otherwise, but it would not be long before Yamaha was fully compensated for their tenacity.

The refocusing of the market on Europe in the middle of the 1960s, encouraged the manufacturers to return to racing on the Old Continent. They only had to slow down momentarily in 1976, when severe anti-pollution measures were imposed on production models, obliging them to assign numerous technicians from the racing department to the development of mass-produced engines.

Yamaha's return : extreme emotions

In 1973, Yamaha once again started participating officially with the Finnish prodigy Jarno Saarinen, 250 World Champion in 1972. The start of the season was dreamlike: Daytona, Imola, Saarinen won these two

Big discovery of the 1975 Season, the young Venezuelan Johnny Cecotto immediately became 350 World champion on a Yamaha TZ very similar to those offered to privateer riders. Cecotto is today automobile racing for BMW.

great classics open to the 750s with his 350 and then linked these to three wins in a row in 250. On the brand new in-line four-cylinder 500, he gained two victories, in France and in Austria. It was the first time since 1967 that the 500 MV-Agustas had been regularly beaten. They had, nevertheless been ridden by the two top stars of the moment, Agostini and Read.

It was not long, however, before the dream was shattered : a multiple fall in 250 at the Italian GP caused the deaths of Pasolini and Saarinen, and Yamaha officially pulled out for the rest of the season.

Sign of the times, Giacomo Agostini left MV-Agusta at the end of 1974 to come and console Yamaha for their tragic previous season. The Italian ace adapted very rapidly to his new two-stroke mounts. Having himself also pocketed Daytona and Imola with the new TZ 750, he won the world 350 title and also snatched the

Giacomo Agostini, after a rich career with MV-Agusta, went over to Yamaha in 1974 and was immediately crowned. Here he is the following year at the 500 Italian GP.

500 title the following year. Yamaha managed to accomplish what Honda had never pulled off, and moreover with a two-stroke : dethroning the unassailable MV-Agustas whose riders had been uninterrupted 500 world champions since 1958 !

Suzuki : the return of the square four

Without doubt attracted by this success, Suzuki also arrived in 1974 with a four-cylinder 500. Even Kawasaki would officially come back to Grand Prix racing the following year. Only Honda, faithful to their public-spirited policy rejected pure speed to devote themselves to such disciplines as Endurance, which they estimated to be more akin to their customers' interests.

With its square four cylinders, Suzuki's RG 500 returned to the architecture of their 250 on the 1960s. But with the 500 Suzuki was far more successful—at its handlebars, Barry Sheene became 1976 World Champion, a title which he would repeat in 1977 up

Englishman Barry Sheene, already extremely popular following his second-place finish in the 125 World Championship of 1971, would bring a great deal to Suzuki with his individual charisma.

Compared to the 250 of the 1960s, the RG 500 of 1974 had integrated one parameter : compactness. The square four cylinders were stacked above the gearbox. The block therefore remained a reasonable length. (drawing M. Nakaoki)

The Yamaha TZ 750, here launched at the 1973 Tokyo Show, swiftly became the unquestioned tool of those wishing to shine in Formula 750. To race in this class, where individuals had in principle been authorized to race with motorcycles derived from production machines, Yamaha had agreed to make a colossal effort : the factory had built a limited series of real racing machines, considered as equivalent to production bikes. The TZ 750, supplied to "private entries" starting in 1974, was in fact very close to the official Grand Prix 500, but it stood out by its valve intake. Its hybrid capacity (700 cc) came from its engine design, basically made up of two TZ 350s in tandem. It developed about one hundred horsepower.

and the Frenchman Patrick Pons in 1979, all on Yamaha OW 31s. The formula was abandoned at this date, following the rise to power of Endurance and the TT Championships.

The great age of Endurance

Always attracted by the categories neglected by the three others, Kawasaki took part in Endurance starting in 1974 by supporting the efforts of Georges Godier and Alain Genoud through the intermediary of their French importer. Since 1973, the 900 Z1 (and its derivatives) had become the absolute for those wanting to feature in such events increasingly appreciated by the public. Godier and Genoud, their machine fitted with a Swiss Egli frame, won the Bol d'Or in 1974, then

against particularly well prepared Yamahas. In this way Suzuki took revenge for the painful disappointments previously inflicted on them in the 250 cc class.

Formula 750

The 750 cc made popular by prestigious non-championship trials was at first only the object of a prize offered by the International Motorcycling Federation, won by Barry Sheene and his Suzuki TR 750 in 1973, then by Johnny Dodds in 1974. Reaching European Championship status, the formula crowned Jack Findlay in 1975 then Victor Palomo in 1976. Like Dodds the previous year, both were riding what was then the ultimate weapon of the private entry, the Yamaha TZ 750. Gary Nixon, on the works Kawasaki H2-R, ought to have won it in 1976, but the cancellation of a dubious event in South America had given the title to the Spaniard. Following its success in this category, a World Championship was created, which rewarded Steve Baker in 1977, Johnny Cecotto in 1978,

Patrick Pons leads from Christian Sarron, both on Yamaha TZ 750 "OW 31" during the 1980 Daytona 200 Miles, which Patrick would be the first Frenchman to win (he remains the only one to this day).

A Swiss Egli frame, a well-prepared Kawasaki engine, good experience in Endurance racing and particularly well managed pit stops in 1974 enabled Georges Godier and Alain Genoud to became the first great specialists in the discipline.

Kawasaki supported the efforts of their importer in 1975 and won the first Endurance championship of Europe. The engine was supplied by the factory, but the bike-frame had been conceived and made in France by a university professor of technology, motorbike mad, who had made maintenance organization easier with one of the first lateral-structure frames. (The machine illustrated here does not have the original swing arm).

again in 1975 with a laterally-structured bike frame with rear single conrod-activated shock absorber, conceived by Pierre Doncque and made in France. During the same meeting, they pocketed the very first European Championship for this speciality with the sponsorship from Xavier Maugendre, at the time Kawasaki importer for France.

Honda in turn took part in 1976, through Honda-France, with the RCB, a machine specially conceived for Endurance. During four years, the pair made up of Christian Léon and Jean-Claude Chemarin would crush any opposition and share in this increasingly popular category, notably in France where the motorcycling Le Mans 24 Hours was launched in 1978.

The temptation of scrambling

From the early 1970s, the Japanese simply could not resist Scrambles, the "soft" discipline of motorbiking. Oddly enough, the first Japanese attempt at Scrambles came from Suzuki. In 1971, the make signed up Gordon Farley to develop a trail bike from their TS 250 trail model. This adventure resulted in the mass-produced RL 250 at the end of 1973, then in its British-style Beamish versions.

Honda launched the 125 Bials in 1972, more for "leisure and rides" than for real competition scrambling. As from 1974, Sammy Miller, 1968 and 1970 European Champion, was signed on for a more serious participation in this discipline which culminated as the TL 250 of 1975. Yamaha entered scrambling in 1973, with a TY 250 which immediately became champion of Japan. The peak of this participation would be Mick Andrew becoming 1971-1972 Champion of Europe

Christian Léon, the great French champion would be four times Endurance champion of Europe, alongside Jean-Claude Chemarin at the handlebars of a Honda RCB (opposite, at the 1976 Barcelona 24 Hours). The 1977 version has been photographed on its stand.

At the end of 1973, the Yamaha TY 250 was fully capable of excellent racing results (where some versions were equipped with fuel injection). Even so, it remained very suitable for ordinary riding, thanks to separate lubrication.

With their KT 250, here in front of Mount Fuji, Kawasaki would not stay long with dirt biking, quickly understanding that this discipline would remain the hunting grounds of the Europeans.

The Suzuki RL 250 dirt bike had only been meeting with a modest success when the English specialist Beamish presented them with a bike frame to measure up to 250 then to 325 cc as from 1977.

on Ossa, which he had developed from the start and which won him the Scottish Six Hours in 1975. Since then, Yamahas have often been seen in scramble racing, but they have never reached the same peak. On the other hand, Yamaha would be the only manufacturer to make a real commercial profit out of scrambling by lowering the TY range to 125, 80, or 50 cc. The TY 125, in particular would break all sales records for scrambler bikes. It was also in 1973 that Kawasaki came into scrambling with Don Smith, 1969 European Champion. This attempt would result in the mass-produced KY 250 of 1975.

All the manufacturers would be disappointed by the lukewarm response of the United States to this type of motorbike, despite American Bernie Schreiber's world title in 1979. The low production runs envisioned for trail bikes turned away the Japanese manufacturers from this style of machine, again leaving the field open to the Spanish and the Italians.

More oriented towards leisure than competition, the little 125 Bials launched by Honda at the end of 1972 was destined more for riding through the countryside than for pure performance.

Higher bidding and implosion

This chapter only covers five years, but five years of bubbling-over for the Japanese motorcycle industry. Production figures reached their peak and everything seemed possible and permissible for manufacturers who sometimes lost their sense of proportion.

Performing better than the Z650 Kawasaki, despite its shaft transmission, the XJ 650 of 1980 stood out by its most elegant strong lines, but also by its remarkably narrow engine, thanks to an alternator placed behind the cylinders. It was rated at 73 hp for 573 lbs. and reached 125 mph, thanks to its minimal frontal area.

n this short lapse of time they would dare everything : machines of an extreme sophistication and unprecedented experimentation, without either follow-up or outcome, everything urgently and without any considered reflection. History would have the task of sorting it out… The market exploded and, profiting from the extraordinary export outlets which were at the same time appearing in the United States, Europe and Japan, Yamaha threw themselves into a frenzied race in pursuit of Honda.

Yamaha cleans out the dead wood

Of the four big manufacturers, Yamaha is the only one never to have run out of steam in their growth : since 1955, they had expanded without the slightest slow-down, with the exception of a little crisis in 1961. They had dislodged Suzuki from second place in 1967, and in 1977, their two-wheeler output was only 25 % lower than that of the number one. So it was that this firm, fearing nothing, boldly announced its objective for the end of the 1970s : to catch up with and then overtake Honda. And, indeed, why not ? Yamaha had just invented the modern day scooter and their Passol made them the "main manufacturer" in Japan. Their enduro ITs were much appreciated in the United States (just like their rivals, Suzuki's PEs) ; their remarkable XT 500 and DT 125MX were doing much for their reputation as well as for their economic health in the fledgling new market that was Europe. On the prestige side, the XS 1100 of 1978 won over all the big road racers of the time. As for racing, this smiled down on them at every starting grid. Yamaha therefore felt at the gates of becoming the historic leader and put all their efforts into an ultimate battle on all fronts to dethrone Hondas.

War was declared, but Honda were the strong ones : in 1978 thanks, among other things, to the automobile, their turnover was close to four times superior to that of Yamaha and they were bristling with pride. Honda would be responding point by point to all Yamaha's provocative strategies.

Yamaha's strokes of genius and clumsiness

Yamaha was overrevving and therefore capable of the best or the worst. The best was of course represented by the excellent XJ 650 and by the marvellous RD 350 LC of 1979.

Well-known for their two-stroke twin race models since the YDS of 1959, Yamaha once again made a big hit at the end of 1979 with their RD 350 LC. This machine,

Sportsmen retain an image of the RD 350 LC as an ultra-efficient machine, not always easy to control, but really charming with its strong personality.

equipped with liquid cooling, was ultra-powerful (47 hp) and weighed only 315 lbs. : this sparked off a fierce debate : was this really making any sense? Obviously the reply was in the negative but what a fabulous toy for a race enthusiast? All those who have ever owned an RD-LC still hold fond memories and Yamaha's reputation finally came out of it the better. This machine would be developed in 1983 with a ver-

sion equipped with YPVS, a system that appeared for racing in 1980 and was composed of a rotary servo valve partially concealing the exhaust, so obtaining a variable diagram. This variant, even more powerful (59 hp), would show itself even easier to exploit and would end up crowning Suzuku king of the two-stroke. The worst were their V-twin cylinders, the 1000 TR1 of 1980 then the XZ550 of 1981. The case history of

these V-twins is painful, because their conceptions were even more interesting and would return in force several years later. The TR1, neither for touring nor racing, equipped with a puzzling style and full of faults would prove a complete fiasco. Technically advanced (liquid cooling, double OHC and four valves per cylinder), but not very attractive with its craggy lines, and fragile without offering the performance of a four cylinder, the

The XZ 550 had above all suffered from unattractive lines, from a carburation difficult to regulate and unimpressive road holding. If Yamaha had only taken the time to refine it, no doubt that it would have found it easier to last longer. The XZ was rated at 64 hp for 412 lbs.

Misunderstood at its launch, the 1000 TR 1 was not lacking in originality with its protected chain crankcase, its luggage carrier and quite simply its upper crate architecture. However, with 70 hp for 485 lbs., this was not a sports model but a safe roadster.

The XV 750 dressed up as a custom bike, took quite a while to find its public, but it anticipated the fashion for custom bikes which dominates today's market. Its later versions (to the left, in 1955) managed to assert themselves in a cylinder range extending from 125 to 1100 cc, under the general label of Virago.

The XLV appeared to have a disturbing style, and in its beginnings suffered from an confused design where undeniable aptitudes for touring were muddled up with three-colored "fire brigade" livery. This XLV took advantage, even if clumsily, of the Paris-Dakar image and its engine introduced the formula of the V-twin with staggered crankpins.

Inspired by the Grand Prix NS, the MVX 250F upturned the cylinder arrangement : two towards the bottom, one at the top. It also adopted an enclosed front disc brake, internally pinched by the caliper from the inside. A 400 cc version of this machine, sold exclusively in Japan, would later become available in Europe as the NS 400R.

XZ met with the same fate. This V-twin should have proved an excellent rival to the Italian Ducatis, like the TRX would fifteen years later. It was merely an ugly machine, a slapdash affair which would cost the make dearly alongside other mistakes of the time.

As for the XV 750, even less remarked on when it came out in 1980, it gave an foretaste of coming fashions in exploiting a Yamaha innovation, the creation of "customized" machines. In 1978 Yahama had in fact been the first Japanese manufacturer to orient themselves along this path with the XS 650 Special, at the same time as Kawasaki with their LTD range.

Honda's implacable reply

The CBX 1000 ought to have set us thinking : with this, Honda entered a period of pure technical delight and enormous activity. Labeled with esoteric acronyms, some of their innovations of the era would survive. Such was the case for ProLink lever suspension, TRAC antidive, the 16-inch front wheel, the staggered crankpin V-twins, the RFVC radial cylinder block or the ATAC two-stokes with auxiliary exhaust chamber. Others would reappear in another form, like the REV variable geometry cylinder block for the CBR 400 in 1983, which would give birth to V-TEC in future automobiles. Others would not in the end get through, such as

the 1978 XLS trail-bike's 23-inch front wheel or the 1981CBX 400/550F's "inboard" disk brakes. This was also an epoch where Honda was innovating on the aesthetic front. In cases like that of the 1983 XLV 750, this was not always very smart, but anyway, at least they risked it! Finally, this was an epoch where Honda launched astonishing models like the MVX 250F, a two-stroke V-three cylinder directly inspired by the

Grand Prix NS : not forgetting the Spacy scooter, clearly futuristic in its first version with retractable headlamp, or the articulated Stream tricycle.

The turbo, symbol of madness

In September 1980, Honda reached the height of sophistication with the CX 500 Turbo. This was certainly not the first motorcycle with electronic fuel injection

Called the XN 85, the Suzuki 650 Turbo hardly should out with its engineering, but its bike-frame demonstrated real progress in that this concerns one of the very first production machines equipped with a 16-inch front wheel. The maneuvrability that came out of this was remarkable for the period. It was rated at 85 hp for 496 lbs.

The Honda CX Turbo was an historically important machine. In use, its engine was lacking in flexibility in its first 500 cc version of 78 hp for 527 lbs. The later 650 version (100 hp for 518 lbs.) was on the other hand a remarkable roadster, sadly suffering beneath the poor reputation of the 500. The 650 is shown here.

(the Kawasaki 100H was ahead by one year) but it was the first representative of the "turbo" generation.

This turbo was a basket into which the three other Japanese would fall : Yamaha, immediately (with a fairly crude version, still fueled by carburettors), Suzuki in 1982, Kawasaki in 1983.

It was quickly proved that an average turbocharged power output, if it was as efficient as a high-powered aspirated one, could be neither more compact nor lighter and that, therefore, its interest remained limited, all the more with its soaring budget.

The CX was nonetheless historically, technically, and aesthetically important. It is said that its original, even if functional, lines with the fuel tank blending in to the side of the streamlining, may have been sketched out by the automobile designer Michelotti. Finally arrived at, the ultimate and very successful CX650 Turbo of 1983

To be able to launch their XJ 650 Turbo at the same time as Honda, Yamaha had to cut short its developmental stage by fitting it out with carburetors and not injection. This machine, with its very angular lines following the trend then in fashion at Yamaha, was hardly more powerful, with its 90 hp for 507 lbs., than a conventional 750.

Out of the four "turbo" motorbikes, the 750 Kawasaki was the most belated but also gave the best performance and whose individuality was the most justified. When it appeared, the poor reputation of the turbo had unfortunately gone before it so there was little chance of profiting from its real advantages. It was rated at 112 hp for 514 lbs.

machine. This monster would not, however, be banking on pure performance : it was instead destined for touring, like the Yamaha XS 1100 and it was indeed for this use that the 1300 Kawasaki gained a worldwide following.

Suzuki invents the modern motorcycle

In this period of frenzy, Suzuki was keeping a cool head. Even better, in 1980 the make was thinking up the lines for the coming decade without anybody being aware of it. It is to Target Design, in Germany, that we owe the Katana range, characterized by several really Teutonic vices (omnipresent grey, stylistic heaviness) but also by strong traits which would come to be copied. The dominant point was created by the dynamic of forward-thrusting lines, which contrasted with

In 1979, the Kawasaki Z 1300 was a superlative motorbike. Very impressive with its volume and weight, this model would be soon equiped with electronic injection in replacement of the three carburettors as shown on this early model.

The Suzuki GSX 1100 S Katana, provocative in its day, later came to be considered as the initiator of a design trend followed by all the manufacturers. It gave out 111 hp for 511 lbs.

came too late to profit from its maturity : the turbo fashion had been but a flash in the pan, rendered disappointing by a generally hasty development, and by a difficult balance between blandness (for the Yamaha and the Suzuki) and a delicate exploitation (for the first Honda and the Kawasaki).

Kawasaki in the big leagues

Without the means to pick up the ever-escalating gauntlets of Honda and Yamaha, Suzuki and Kawasaki reduced their activities to wait for calmer days. This did not prevent them from making the effort.
Kawasaki were totally excessive with their Z 1300, launched in the autumn of 1978. This was the biggest (1,268 cc), the heaviest (652 lbs), and the most powerful (120 hp) of the Japanese motorbikes. But to cap it all, there was the Honda CBX, the only six-cylinder

the horizontal or backward-sloping lines known until then. This forward transfer would be further accentuated as from 1983 by the 16-inch wheels. Today one can clearly distinguish between "before" and "after" Katana motorcycles. An entire symbolic design, without doubt excessive in its time, but which, in the year 2000 was still available (in Japan) from the Suzuki catalogue!

Hard return to reality

In the short term, the European and Japanese markets, artificially boosted by an unending fireworks display of novelties, took off. This little game was not, however, without risk. The models would come out hastily prepared, they would mutually outmode each other in a few months and finish by ruining their manufacturers in research costs, in after-sales(in the management and storage of parts) then in marketing and promotion. No sooner out than these models were sold off cheaply, to the despair of the dealers who entered into a fratricidal war for survival.

Before long the customer would lose interest in this escalation and the house of cards would collapse with Yamaha throwing in the towel.

This crisis of 1981-1982 was a major one for Yamaha, for whom the motorbike still made up over two thirds

of their turnover (only 30% with Honda and Suzuki). One further aggravating circumstance : since the second oil crisis in 1979, the price of gas had doubled on the still crucial US market. Certainly, the fall in the yen and the rise in the dollar between 1980 and 1985 ought to have favored exports. But this would not take into account the protectionism that was becoming a reality in certain countries.

With the automobile, the Japanese even preferred to impose voluntary restrains for the US begenning in 1981 : they would reach 25% of the market share in 1980 and this preventive self-censorship would last until 1994.

Elsewhere they were faced with quotas : 3% of the automobile market in France (from 1978 to 1993) ; two thousand two hundred cars per year in Italy. And for the motorbike, Japanese models of less than 380cc were banned from Italy until the 1980s.

It should be said that, for a long time, a bone of contention had existed over the textile industry between Italy and Japan. Suddenly, the Italians took their revenge even though there were no more import duties in Japan since 1978.

In short, Japan was becoming annoying, in so far as her domination had become indecent : and this rude behavior even if artificial, was not immediately apparent.

Some rays of sunshine, all the same

Parallel to this unbridled growth that led to this harsh crisis, hope remained for those who knew how to analyze the market in all its excesses. This hope was symbolized by three trends, on which the manufacturers would know how to make a quick comeback.

Sand Enduro, which had been attracting over one thousand riders on the beach at Le Touquet (since 1975) and above all the great Paris-Dakar adventure (as of 1979), proved that the general public was still interested in the motorbike, provided it made them dream and helped them to escape the humdrum of daily life.

The customized school (launched in 1978 by Yamaha and Kawasaki with models distributed through the US) proved that there existed, even in Europe, a market for wholesome machines, even if a little showy, but illustrating a new motorbiking approach, more laid back, less aggressive, which evoked the American "choppers", and by extension, the American way of life.

The return of the scooter had been initiated by Yamaha in Japan in 1977. And Japan discovered to their amazement that, for the first time, it had issued more driving licences to women than to men : the myth of the macho country suffered a blow!

In 1982, it was at the controls of this machine, a derivative of the XL 500R, that Cyril Neveu won the Paris-Dakar rally.

The famous Yamaha vertical twin discovered a new lease on life in 1978 with this XS 650 Special version re-clothed as a custom bike (here photographed in 1979). Custom bikes more influenced by Harley-Davidson and equipped with V-twin engines would soon be making their appearance.

16-inch wheels, egg-shaped bike-frame in aluminium sheeting, lateral radiators, engine with oblong pistons and eight valves per cylinder, the first NR undoubtedly innovated a little too much. Here it is at the 1979 French GP, in the hands of Takazumi Katayama.

Open heart view of the NR engine. One realizes that this is in reality a fake V8 with eight inlet manifold, eight spark plugs and those incredible oblong cylinders.

Racing : the escalation

In racing as on the industrial front, Japanese manufacturers were living out a period of euphoria. Honda were delirious and even Kawasaki, for the first time (and indeed for the last) took part in Grand Prix racing.

The end of the Honda NR

Announced at the end of 1977, the return of Honda to Grand Prix racing with a four-stroke became the symbol of this somewhat mad epoch. Their NR 500 was unveiled in the summer of 1979. Here was a V4 with oblong pistons, with two conrods per piston, two spark plugs per cylinder, and eight valves per combustion chamber. In short it was a V8 whose pistons had been soldered two-by-two to meet with Grand Prix regulations, which banned "over four cylinders". Nor was the chassis lacking : the pressed steel hull enclosed the engine from the outside, the radiators were lateral and the wheels were 16 inches in diameter.

In the hands of Mick Grant and Takazumi Katayama (who had become the first Japanese World Champion, in 1977, on a 350 Yamaha), the NR had disastrous beginnings in England and France, before leaving to pur-

The NR, in production beginning in 1991, was meant to be the most élite on the market. Its price was the best guarantee of its exclusivity, but its performance was no better than that of a conventional 750.

The engine of the 1987 750 NR, a racing V8 thirty years after the 500 Moto Guzzi.

been considerably developed, with a completely conventional chassis, but its performance was scarcely better than those of a "normal" RVF. This would be the only European race for this NR 750, with wich the Australian Mal Campbell would nevertheless win a heat of the Swan Series in November.

There was price to pay for this half-baked image : when they presented the production NR (quite simply) at the end of 1991, Honda met with great difficulty in selling its stock. Completely logical, and finally normal enough for a sportingly unsuccessful 750 cc, priced at $ 56,300, while a VFR750F with similar performance itself cost less than $ 9,000 !

The Kawasaki KR oust the Yamaha TZs

When it first made its appearance at the start of the 1975 season in the US, with Yvon Duhamel at the controls, the KR 250 surprised. The machine's architecture astonished, with its two cylinders in tandem, and here was the first time that Kawasaki openly participated in speed ; the factory had hardly supported Simmonds when it won him his 125 title in 1960. The tuning was a little laborious but an initial Grand Prix came in 1977 with Mick Grant. No less than eight world titles in 250 and 350 would follow between

sue its private entry development in Japan. By 1980, its chassis had become a little more conventional (18-inch wheels, then tubular frame) but the efficiency was still not up to scratch. The machine reappeared in 1981, but only gained superficial non-championship victories. It must be said that, for the first time in Grand Prix history, the three other Japanese manufacturers were also present in this 500 category. And, after three new Grand Prix attempts at the start of 1982, the NR 500 slipped away for good. A new NR 500 later put in appearance at various trade shows in 1984. It had been fitted with a frame and rocker arm in carbon fiber, but

would never race in this trim. At the same time there was talk of an NR250 Turbo, a half-NR 500 whose two cylinders would be boosted by twin turbochargers. This engine would never get past the test bench stage. The monster against surfaced in April 1987 to take part in the Le Mans 24 Hours in 750cc. The machine had

The KR 250 and 350 would unashamedly dominate these two classes from 1978 to 1982, thanks to their excellent chassis as well as to the talents of their various riders such as Jean-François Baldé, at the 1982 French GP. The stripped-down version is from 1976.

Kork Ballington at the controls of the KR 500 would only obtain a few successes during his three seasons in 500 Grand Prix. The over-innovative bike-frame of this machine was without doubt responsible for this failure. Here is the first 1980 version (below) with the 1982 version in front of the present home of Ken Suzuki (team manager at the time).

1978 and 1982 for Kork Ballington and Anton Mang, practically without any further development. Rarely did a machine meet with such strong and longlasting

supremacy, and the KR would make its mark on all those who had the chance to try it out. Thanks to the influence which Xavier Maugendre, importer for France had with the factory, many Frenchmen would enjoy this privilege, and Jean-François Baldé would be the one who came nearest to the supreme title.

Overcome by the exhilaration of the moment, between 1980 and 1982 Kawasaki even participated in 500. This would be the only period in history when the Big Four would be officially present in the same class. This 500, sadly, would be the only false note of the beautiful KR adventure. In three years, it would be almost totally unsuccessful despite (or because of?) its most original hull-frame technology.

At the end of 1989, then again since 1993, there have been a few sporadic appearances by a new 250 Kawasaki in the Japanese Championship and in several American races, but without any great success so far.

Suzuki and Kawasaki reap the benefit

While the two leaders were marking time in the development of the new Grand Prix V4 concept (as a four-stroke for Honda, as a two-stroke for Yamaha), Suzuki, pragmatic, gained two world titles in 500 with Lucchinelli (1981) then Uncini (1982), thanks to a square-four that was at the end of its development but assured and seasoned.

For their part, the young riders Fontan and Moineau finished by putting an end to the supremacy of Léon and Chemarin in that entirely separate speciality which had become Endurance, so presenting the first world title in this discipline to Honda and to their RCB in 1980. However Kawasaki wrenched the title from them in 1981 (with Roche and Lafond) and 1982 (with Chemarin and Cornu), thanks to KR 1000s which were far more adept at the series than the Honda RCBs.

Randy Mamola (Suzuki - N°10) and Marco Lucchinelli (Suzuki - N°2) leading Kenny Roberts (Yamaha - N°1) during the 500 British Grand Prix in 1980. "Lucky" would become world champion the following year.

Inset :
The 1982 world champion. Suzuki had merely refined a formula launched in 1974. Opposite the all-out research of Honda and Yamaha, this strategy proved worthwhile. Kawasaki reclaimed the Endurance throne in 1981 with this 1000. The chassis was built in Japan at the command of the French racing stable, Performance.

Yamaha rides on a wave of success

Three 500 titles in a row for Kenny Roberts from 1978 to 1980 might have persuaded Yamaha into believing that they had reached their goal. Was the illusion of a Honda at their heels perhaps in part due to the enthusiasm of the moment, even though the leader was getting bogged down in the development of their NR 500? The performance of "King Kenny" was not any less admirable faced with such fierce rivalry, made up of several finely tuned Yamahas and Suzukis. Since Agostini, nobody had dominated this king of classes like him.

Kenny Roberts, arriving in Europe in 1977, carried a new style of riding in his baggage. Raised in the dirt-track school of controlled skidding, the American rider gave a new rhythm to Grand Prix racing. Here he is at the 1979 French Grand Prix.

Even on three wheels

The side-car fraternity, in short supply of engines after the BMW Rennsports and then the Königs had run out, found engineering which suited them in the TZ 500. From 1977 to 1987, without interruption, this Yamaha engine became world side-car champion, a use which had certainly not been envisioned for it at the beginning ! This engine would only be outmoded in 1988, by a Krauser whose design would be very similar to the TZ 500.

The Frenchman Alain Michel only became world side-car champion in 1990, but he had spent a large part of his career at the handlebars of Yamaha-engined link-ups like this LCR in 1982.

Kawasaki again won the constructors title in 1983, but it was Hubin and Moineau who clinched the driver title for Suzuki, with a GS 1000 R, itself very close to the production model. Even so, a disappointing period followed and, at the end of 1982, Yamaha, Suzuki, and Kawasaki pulled out of the Grand Prix, which had become too costly in a period of harsh recession. Incorrigible, Suzuki and Yamaha would however return as quickly with the financial support and under the colors of the major cigarette manufacturers.

The Dakar adventure

Thierry Sabine had been organizing the Enduro des Sables at Le Touquet since 1975. Jean-Claude Berrand had been organizing the Ivory Coast-French Riviera rally since 1977. These two events enjoyed a really popular success, so Thierry Sabine ended up by organizing the Paris-Dakar in January 1979. It was a real godsend for the press who had nothing to get their teeth into at this time of the year, as it was for the riders for whom the off season was sometimes empty.

Cyril Neveu win the first two "Dakars" in 1979 and 1980 on a 500 Yamaha XT that earned its spurs : all the ex-hippie roadsters rediscovered their youth on this hardy but very updated machine.

Delirium even in moto-cross

The transitional period of the 1980s was a period of folly for scrambles : in 1980, for the first time, the three world titles, 125, 250, and 500 cc, reverted to Japanese machines. It was a period which favored technical development, and where suspension was particularly cared for, with a variety of rear lever systems. Honda came to the Japanese Championship with a 125 fitted with parallalogram-type fork, of the Ribi type, and even a 125 twin (only Gilera and CZ would do the same in Europe). Neither of these two machines would take part in the World Championship, but they well illustrate an epoch where everything, really everything, seemed possible.

Franck Gross and Pierre-Etienne Samin gave the Suzuki GS 1000 R one of its first great Endurance wins at the 1980 Bold'Or. Fine tribute to the late Jean-Bernard, who had been the craftsman behind the make's arrival at this discipline and would be succeeded by the talented Dominique Méliand.

The 500 XT victorious at Dakar in 1979 and 1980 was still very close to its production version : only forks and fuel tank were clearly different.

This machine perfectly symbolized Honda's experimental way of thinking at the beginning of the 1980s. It would win a heat of the Japanese Championship in 1981.

Rounding off the angles

The Japan of the 1980s had become extremely powerful. In its financial "bubble",
in 1985 it became the second richest country in the world in terms of gross national product.
Twenty years before, this GNP was only just superior to that of Greece.

*The VF 750F was certainly not the first Honda V4, but this was the bike which would really get the formula going. Alongside the Suzuki XN85,
this machine was one of the first to adopt a 16-inch front wheel, and its handling was extraordinary for its time. It is rated at 86 hp for 480 lbs.*

The motorcycle crisis of around 1980 was not any less harsh. Two-wheeler output in Japan would be practically divided by three between 1981and 1987, returning to the 1970 levels, and exports by four from 1981 to 1989.

Following a severe reprimand, the Big Four returned to reason, more or less. This cure took diverse forms, but consisted in all of them toning down the steamroller effect of previous years to calm the protectionist temptations of their "client" countries.

This latter risk was not insignificant : as from April 1983 an importation surtax in the US hit the over 700 cc machines, those which, as if by chance, particularly threatened the Harley-Davidsons. And because of the fall of the dollar (which between February 1985 and October 1987 passed from two hundred and sixty to one hundred and thirty yen), exports of Japanese motorbikes into the United States, still over one million units in 1981, would fall under the two hundred thousand mark in 1990.

Building on the consumer markets

To turn this problem around, from then on the Big Four tried to manufacture where they were selling and to leave the rest so that local industry could regain a little power. The production of the SKD or CKD ("Semi" or "Completely Knocked Down"), with these machines being exported from Japan in spare parts then assembled abroad, came close to four hundred thousand units in 1987, then seven hundred thousand in 1988 and 1989. It had been oscillating between one hundred and two hundred thousand annual units since 1980. This gain, spectacular though it was, did not make up for production losses in Japan.

A strong consolidation in Europe followed. In Spain, it was the buy-out of Montesa by Honda in 1982, of Puch by Suzuki in 1983, of Sanglas by Yamaha in 1987 and even the conclusion of business agreements between Kawasaki and Derbi. In Italy, it was the creation of Honda-Italy in 1977, followed by industrial agreements between Yamaha and their importer Belgarda, then the engine builder Minarelli. In France, it was at last technical agreements between Honda and Peugeot in 1982, then the buy out of MBK by Yamaha in 1984. There were also take overs of every kind, like that of English tire manufacturer Dunlop by the Sumitomo

Group in 1984 or that of Swedish suspension manufacturer Öhlins by Yamaha. The final measure of the integration of Japan into its target markets was the technical support of local industry : sale of engines to Bimota then Aprilia, KTM, and MüZ, technical assistance for Cagiva in Grand Prix racing, strong Japanese presence in the latest Triumphs, suspension and carburetor supply to Harley-Davidson etc.

Rebirth, despite everything

Along with this return to reason, came the rise to power of the scooter. "Reinvented" by Yamaha in 1977, the scooter invaded Europe as of 1983 and would never go out of fashion despite the wearing of a helmet being legally required in Japan in 1986. An understandable safety precaution, but dissuasive enough for many neophytes attracted by the practical side of city motorbiking. The manufacturers would respond to this measure by installing a helmet box on the majority of their models. Another measure, harmful on the face of it, was the limitation to one hundred horsepower, that gained ground

in Europe (Germany then France) in the middle of the decade. Despite this handicap, which killed off the high-powered dream machines on the two biggest European markets of 1986 the market would make a recovery in the majority of western countries.

Honda behaves like a leader

To come out best from this troubled period, Honda employed several strategies. At first, to make a clean sweep of this bygone period, they invented a new breed of engine : the V4. Of course, this was a configuration that had been around for a long time, but which had not often been exploited in the motorcycle. Honda would adapt it for all possible purposes.

At the end of 1981 they presented their production VF 750S and in March 1982 entered a 1000 FWS for the Daytona race. Wasn't the former convincing enough? And the latter, didn't it win the race ? No matter, Honda had ways of insisting. And their VF 750F launched at the end of 1982, would be a total success commercially and technically, immediately backed up by race suc-

At the start of the 1980s, Honda was busy on all fronts and even attacked the niche market for prestige motorbikes, until then the reserve of the Bimota and other European productions. Their CB 1100R of 1981, costly and exclusive, devoted great care to both finish and to detail. This tradition would be carried on in the second version of the 1100R in 1982, then the VF1000R in 1984 and finally the RC 30 and RC 45.

As at the beginning of the 1970s, rivalry had no other alternative than to fall in line with trends launched by Honda. Yamaha then Suzuki launched V4s in 1984, both in the form of big roadsters to compete with the Gold Wing. The 1200 (then 1300 cc) Yamaha Venture and the 1400 Suzuki Cavalcade would however prove bitter failures. Yamaha would recuperate its tooling with the V-Max, Suzuki would not even manage to get rid of their stocks of 700 and 1200 Maduras, custom bikes also equipped with this V4 engine.

cesses from the NSR 500 (1985 world champion) and RS 850 (victorious at the Bold'Or in the autumn of 1983). The V4 strategy, maturing gradually, patiently constructed, would assure Honda of a definite and long-lasting supremacy, and when Yamaha and Suzuki in turn embarked on the V4 adventure, it would not be with ease and even smacked of follow-my-leader.

Yamaha refuse to accept defeat

Yamaha, upset by its tumble, was not discouraged. From the end of 1982, the make made a comeback with two models, stringently developed but which would meet with a very great success in Europe, the XJ 900 and the XT 600W Ténéré. The first was a great road ve-

hicle, descendent of the XJ 650. The second installed a engine close to the XT 550 into a cycle-frame evocative of an entry for the Paris-Dakar, whose popularity had never stopped growing.

Re-assured by these two successes, the manufacturer became bolder the following year and launched three, more ambitious models, the FJ 1100, RD 500 LC and 1200 V-Max. The FJ 1100, worked out by a European team, was exclusively conceived for the old continent. Its frame configuration would set a trend by laterally enclosing the engine instead of turning it round from above. The RD 500 LC, with a more international role, was nothing less than a replica of the Grand Prix 500s, equipped with a V4 two-stroke engine. With almost 90 hp for 390 lbs., the machine would restore—if need be—Yamaha's image in the super-sports sector. With regained confidence, Yamaha also expressed themselves within their American branch, which developed a 1200V-Max, more specifically aimed at the United States. With its 145 hp, this V4-engined monster was the most powerful production motorcycle in the world. With its tough appearance, halfway between a dragster and a custom, it would also do much to restore Yamaha's reputation. No one manufacturer would dare to adventure into its domain for a long while. Finally Yamaha completed their return to the top with their FZ 750 in September 1984. Its inclined twenty-valve four-

The XT 600 Z Ténéré was the first machine to take advantage of the Paris-Dakar niche. Its development had not been expensive: the engine came from the existing XT 550 with its four valves and twin carbs. Its immense suspension clearances and its 30-liter tank turned it into an impressive machine. France, then Italy, would give it a warm welcome, seduced by its prestigious reputation for its potential for long distance runs or for off-road riding.

Although not very expensive to develop as its engine was taken out of the XJ 650 and 750, the XJ 900 would be much appreciated by the big European bikers. Its elegant curvaceous lines would not appear foreign. Its success would be extended as of 1993 by the Diversion 900, offering the same advantages in a updated form.

With its two 16-inch wheels, its huge tires, its lateral frame, and its very typical lines, the FJ 1100 would make its mark on the period and enjoy a long and happy career. Its performance was worthy of the best racing bikes of the time : it pushed out 125 hp for 500 lbs. But its qualities as a big roadster would also be appreciated by hardened European bikers and it would soon be transformed into a real GT. At the end of 1990, its 1200 cc version would become the first Japanese motorcycles with ABS braking.

The RD 500 LC, everybody dreamed of it, Yamaha had dared to do it. The engine had an astonishing architecture : front cylinder intake was by valves below-engine, while that of the upper cylinders was with valves in the cylinders themselves. The Japanese version had a alloy frame, the European version being content with a more sturdy steel frame.

Initially developed for the United States, the 1200 Yamaha V-Max would have some success, but would above all seduce France, which would not hesitate in becoming its almost exclusive customer. Its totally outrageous lines, half-dragster/half custom, linked it to no one school, placing it on the fringes of world output.

Its lines were clumsy, but the FZ 750 is merited with having introduced five-valve technology and inclined cylinders.

cylinder engine was as efficient as reliable, but the fashion was already for machines with a more sporting appearance. The FZ, which was only partially streamlined and without double-optic headlamp, would not carry the same weight as the Suzuki GSX-R.

Kawasaki still playing on the edge

At the end of 1983, Kawasaki hit hard with their GPZ 900 Ninja. True to form, the firm had created a model that cut right across all the others. First in its frame, constituted of a backbone above the engine, without lower cradles. Also in its engine, the make's first four-valve multi-cylinder (the single cylinder KLR trail bike preceded it by a few months), which stood out by its chain-drive at the end of the crankshaft and by the presence of balance pendulums. Very rapidly, the Ninja would establish itself as the new sporting reference,

not as much by its pure power ("almost" 115 hp) than by its relative compactness in comparison to other high-powered machines of the time (503 lbs). A real

innovator, the Ninja would open the way to a long series of 1000 cc and 1100 cc high performance Kawasakis.

Ten years after its launch, the Ninja would still appear in the Kawasaki catalogue, an exceptional longevity for a pure race model, originally meant to have been rapidly phased out! Is design was completely innovative, with its backbone frame (without lower cradles). Its engine with distributive drive at the end of the crankshaft and shaft balance also heralded a new generation of in-line four-cylinder powerplants. The whole machine would moreover influence a new generation of Triumphs.

Suzuki invents the "hyper-sport" generation

In the autumn of 1984, Suzuki created such an event as only those who have for a long time remained isolated and silent know how to do. The revolution, because it was indeed such, was the fact of two really different machines, but whose formulae were similar: hi-tech power and feather weight in the service of an exacerbated sportsmanship. As it happened, the GSX-R 750 put out 100 hp for 388 lbs. (sixty pounds less than a Yamaha FZ),and the RG 500 Gamma claimed 95 hp for 340 lbs. (a good forty-five pounds less than an RD 500 LC).

How had Suzuki managed this? By refining the concept of these two machines down to the smallest detail, in going back to basics over the function of each part, in trying to combine these functions as much as possible (with, for the GSX-R, engine cooling using lubricating oil), in calling on new materials and assembly techniques (aluminium frames combining extruded with cast sections), but also in calculating just right and in particular sacrificing the charm of daily use.

In 1983, the RG 250 Gamma was the first production motorbike of modern times with an aluminium frame. Essentially aimed at the Japanese market, this ultra-light (289 lbs) and powerful (45 hp) machine would not be strange in the dynasty of the 250 racing Suzukis since the 1950s. It is here presented by the 500 World Champion in 1982, Franco Uncini.

Undoubtedly, one of the most important machines of the 1980s, the first GSX-R 750 had pared down the final ounces in every detail of its conception, even to the extent of eliminating the central kickstand. Without doubt it had gone too far in this direction : its subsequent versions agreed to take on weight to guarantee a sufficient rigidity and a better reliability.

More finished than the RD 500LC, Suzuki's RG 500 Gamma would only have one fault : to appear after the Yamaha. Its technology was both noble (with its four rotary valves) but purged, less uselessly complex. It remained the last representative of the "GP replicas".

In fact the GSX-R proved disappointing to use and would rapidly have to put on weight to offer sufficient rigidity and reliability. As for the Gamma, it would not meet with the same public response as had the RD-LC : Suzuki's image, a little lackluster, would come out rejuvenated, but the Gamma would not be a great commercial success.

The GSX-R, on the other hand, would prove a sensation. Above all, it would open up the way to an entire line of "hyper-sport" machines from all the manufacturers. These motorcycles, increasingly removed from ordinary highway use, were forever uncomfortable and unreasonable, but built up a really strong image.

The method would again prove a formula ten years later, when the Honda CBR 900RR Fireblade would at the end of 1995 celebrate its sixty thousand units sold during a span of only four years.

Direct descendant of the GSX-R, representing exactly the same formulae, the Fireblade would however have a sacred handicap : by this time, Germany and above all France would have instigated a power output limitation of 100 hp for motorcycles, causing these machines, so powerful in their "unlimited" version, to lose a big part of their magic.

The Suzuki Intruder (here in its 1400 version) was the elegant culmination of the "soft chopper" school. Instead of the overloaded show-bike, its pure lines played the spartan custom bike. Curiously, it would be coolly received in the United States but better appreciated in Japan and Europe.

More reasonable, but still just as seductive

The order of the day was "round off the angles", just as much for the markets, suspected of protectionism, as for the customers themselves. In the middle of the 1980s, the manufacturers understood that it was in their interest to take a "civic" turn, responsible, where both governments and the governed were concerned. But the mistake made some ten years before would not be repeated. No more a question of turning out emasculated and insipid motorbikes: the manufacturers had

Born as a purely racing machine, the VFR 750F would soon become the joy of those loving high-speed touring when, hidden behind its pure performance, they discovered its comfort, its reliability, and its great versatility.

Even though they had not been the pioneer of the four-stroke big single (its SP 370 only appeared in 1978) Suzuki would harvest a big turnover, particularly with their DR 600 of 1985. Above all, they would end up offering the biggest single on the market with this DR 750 in 1988, then its 800 version (precisely 779 cc) in 1990. The DR "Big" would stand out by its colors and its very particular front "beak".

In the middle of the 1980s, there was a market demand for, if not for toned-down, at least for softened machines. The CBRs (600 and here 1000 cc) were perfectly in phase with this trend, with their generously curved bodywork totally enclosing the engineering. To achieve this, Honda had taken one step back, but the CBR 600F would celebrate its two hundred thousandth unit in 1995, a really incredible figure for such a radical sports model.

With its 600 cc V-twin, the Transalp offered an interesting alternative to the big single 600 cc trail bikes. It would seduce many hardened bikers, but also many citizens, with its reasonable saddle height, its overall softness, and its great ease in use.

By launching the 1000 GTR, Kawasaki clearly showed their colors : nothing would come anywhere near it for five years. A way of telling the buyer in advance that their investment would not depreciate prematurely. In fact, even today this machine gives pleasure to the regular riders allergic to BMWs and at reasonable price. Here is the 1992 version.

from now on perfectly understood that the motorcycle seduced by its image of freedom, by its savage aspect and that it was a question of looking after that aspect… with machines objectively made more reasonable.

Numerous models that first appeared in the 1980s are still with us fifteen years afterwards as witness to the correctness of this appreciation.

This was the case for completely different types such as the Honda Transalp (1986) and Africa Twin (1988), the Kawasaki GTR (1985) and ZZR(1990) or the Suzuki LS650 (1986), not forgetting the lower-powered or customized machines.

A common point for all these models : the respect for the user, the will to re-assure him with the most long-lasting, most practical, but above all the least innovative machines.

The temptation of the hybrid

Fatally, the return to sound values and to softened motorbikes would also bring about a revival of the old historic myth about the motorbike that wanted to look like a scooter or a two-wheeled car.

Honda would be the one who followed this path most seriously, with its CN 250 Spazio scooter(end of 1986) then with their PC 800 Pacific Coast (1988) ; Suzuki would follow, in a "retro" form, with their 250

The CN 250 Spazio is a mutant scooter, high-powered (in Japan the 125s do not have access to the highways or expressways) whose armchair-saddle is evocative of custom bikes. It appears particularly generous in its dimensions and in its storage areas. Coming out in Japan in 1986, it was not exported into Europe until 1988, but this was still too early. The Spazio only attracted Italy and Switzerland and it was not until the middle of the 1990s that the success of the big scooter would spread to the rest of Europe.

SW-1. As it ought to, the concept was given a cold reception, because it was as puzzling as ever, but it ended up a success. Ten years after its birth, the Spazio is not only still in the catalogue, but it was copied by the 250 Yamaha Majesty. As for the Pacific Coast, expensive to produce and costly to buy, its fans miss it terribly and

have been flushing out the last remaining examples as far as the United States where its lack of success meant stock accumulating at the dealers.

The case of the SW-1, more marginal by definition, was only trivial, but one day without any doubt we will see this type of machine again.

Spazio and the Pacific Coast were in the same vein. As might be expected, the idea did not immediately catch on with the Old Continent: as the target buyers for this type of machine did not necessarily have a motorbike permit, the market was fatally limited. The customers of the PC would be only too happy to have at last found a decent and roomy machine, in short a scooter with the performance of a motorbike, but without the belittling aspect of a scooter.

In the moto/automobile family, Suzuki also decided to play the nostalgic card and to follow the new fashion with their SW-1. Was it its "fashion victim" aspect which did a disservice to this machine, or its really over-peculiar appearance ? That it was expensive to make certainly limited its distribution. Presented as a V-twin at the end of 1989, it was finally produced as a single in 1992.

With its 750 cc twin, with two inclined cylinders and five valves per cylinder, the super Ténéré really played out the Paris-Dakar card. It would not, however, reach the same turnover as its rival.

Initially developed from the Transalp, as a 650 cc, the Africa Twin would quickly take on a more "Dakar" shape. The career of its 750 cc development would be bolstered by wins from the NXR in this rally and cause a considerable stir.

Perfume of Africa

With the Honda XRV 650 Africa Twin (end of 1987), then the Yamaha XTZ 750 Super Ténéré (end of 1988), the sands of Africa invaded Europe. These rugged twin-cylinder trail bikes, heavy and powerful, were ill at ease as scramblers, but appeared as honest roadsters when compared to the "hyper-sports" which were beginning to invade the market.

They evidently picked up the image forged in the Paris-Dakar by the Honda NXRs of Neveu, Lalay, and Orioli since 1986. The reputation of rallying was then at its peak but it would not be long in declining, and Yamaha would no longer be able to fully exploit the later victories of Peterhansel.

The duel continues

In 1982, embarrassed by an NR which chroniclers have baptized "Never Ready",
Honda changed their tactics and launched the NS 500 into Grand Prix racing.

Freddie Spencer and the three-cylinder NS 500,
an entire symbol since 1983 of a new generation of motorcycles and a new generation of riders.

Nor was it humdrum in any way. Contrary to the four-cylinder configuration which was the norm of the time, the NS was a V3 like the German DKWs of the 1950s: one almost horizontal cylinder, two vertical cylinders. The fuel supply to this very compact engine passed through the intermediary of valves and not rotary feeders. Less powerful but lighter than its rivals, the NS also demanded a different approach to riding with its 16-inch front wheel and its very particular geometry, adapted to the style of its rider, Freddie Spencer.

At the time of one of the most epic duels in the history of the 500 class, which kept Suzuki at a respectable distance, Spencer and the NS finished by dominating Roberts' Yamaha at the end of the 1983 season : Honda had at last achieved its aim, seventeen years after Hailwood's semi-failure with the RC 181. The following year, Eddie Lawson replaced Roberts at Yamaha and

The rider of the second half of the 1980s was Eddie Lawson. He would be four-time World Champion in 500, before going over to Indy Formula auto-racing. Here he is in 1986 chasing his first title for Yamaha.

avenged the affront of 1983 by taking advantage of Spencer's problems with the latest NSR.

This V4-engined NSR stood out with its unique crankshaft (its competitors had two of them), its fuel tank shoe under the engine and its exhausts in the usual position of the fuel tank. Direct consequence : the machine's performance improved as the tank emptied, requiring great delicacy to make it efficient at the start as well as the finish of the race.

Honda adjusted its sights for 1985 by returning the exhausts and the fuel tank back to their normal configuration. Spencer, at the peak of his form, wiped away any competition in 500, as well as in 250, to bring an end to the domination, since 1982, of the private entry or semi- private entry Yahamas in this class.

Honda had in fact developed a new V-twin which made sure of the double with Spencer and Mang. Spencer's

In 1982 then 1984, it was respectively Jean-Louis Tournardre and Christian Sarron who would clinch the 250 World Championship at the controls of Yamaha TZ. In this way they consoled the French for the previous dark period of 1980-1981 which had seen the successive fatalities of Chevalier, Pons, Léon, Peyré, and Rougerie.

double title was a genuine achievement given the level reached in racing modern motorcycles which demanded very precise tuning, and studious trials in a time long past the days when Hailwood and Redman could win three different classes in one day on the same mount ! Spencer would however pay for this the following year. Nervously exhausted, physically drained, he cracked up at the first Grand Prix and had to withdraw without putting up the slightest resistance ; Lawson's Yamaha pocketed the title.

He would never return to his previous level. In 250, it was the new Yamaha V-twin of Lavado which celebrated the official comeback of the factory to the class, by outstripping the Honda of Sito Pons.

In 1987, the Australian Gardner took over for Honda and walked off with the 500 title opposite the Yamahas of Mamola and Lawson. In 250, total domination of the Hondas of Mang, Roth, Pons, and Sarron : Wimmer's Yamaha was only seventh. Gardner's title was announced with perfect timing, as the manufacturers were refocusing their acitivities on the Asia-Pacific zone : the event would meet with considerable acclaim in the Antipodes.

In 1988, Lawson took revenge and led Gardner (Honda) and Rainey (Yamaha) in 500, while the Honda of Sito Pons led Garriga's Yamaha in 250.

In 1989 at last, Lawson transferred to Honda and won his fourth 500 title, perhaps his finest, in front of Rainey's Honda. Since Agostini, nobody had won more than three titles in 500. In 250, Sito Pons this time outstripped a trio of Honda's ridden by Roth, Cornu, and Cardus.

Endurance, a particularly French speciality

For their two world Endurance titles of 1981 and 1982, Kawasaki had confidence in the Performance workshops of Serge Rosset. When Moineau and Hubin snatched away this title in 1983, it was on a Suzuki, also prepared by a French racing stable, that of Dominique Méliand.

In 1984, when the maximum cubic capacity in this discipline had been reduced from 1000 to 750 cc and Honda returned with their V4, it was quite naturally Honda France who were charged by the factory to looked after the official machines. Patrick Igoa and Gérard Coudray would give them three consecutive titles, before Hervé Moineau regained recognition for Suzuki in 1987 (with Bruno Le Bihan) and 1988 (with Thierry Crine).

At the end of the 1980s, Endurance was still very prized in France : the Bol d'Or and the Le Mans 24 Hours were still the formula. Faced with the loss in popularity of this discipline around the rest of the world, the FIM finished by withdrawing its world status and Alex Vieira had to be content in 1989 and 1990 with a simple "FIM Cup" on his Kawasaki.

Hervé Moineau leads Pierre-Etienne Samin during the 1982 Le Mans 24 Hours, but it was the latter who would win the race. The former would make up for it by becoming World Champion the following year.

The Superbikes, heirs of Formula TT

The British, very influential at the FIM, had managed to create a "Formula TT" when their Tourist Trophy, considered as too dangerous by the riders, had been moved away from Grand Prix racing. From 1977 to 1986, this formula had awarded world titles without any great significance. But having grown in size, as of 1987, this category ended up provoking the setting-up of a World Superbike Championship in 1988.

It was at the controls of this GSX-R 750 that Hervé Moineau became for the fourth and last time World Endurance champion in 1988, so making him the most titled French rider in history.

The Basque Patrick Igoa would be three times world champion at the handlebars of Honda RVFs. Here he is in 1986 during his last title season.

This Championship, reserved for 750 cc four-strokes (or 1000 cc for the twin cylinders), took advantage of machines close to those available on the market, and was not slow in meeting with success, with Fred Merkel winning the first two contests for Honda. Favored by the regulations, the Ducati twins from then on dominated the formula.

The Superbike formula (as well as its derived formula, the Supersports, reserved for 600 cc and twin-cylinders of 750 cc) has continued to grow ever since, and the four Japanese manufacturers are all there, officially entered alongside Ducati and Aprilia.

Cross wins its spurs

The green motorbike was at the height of its popularity in France during the 1980s. The specialised press was created and Supercross was very successfully organized at Bercy. This craze was without doubt linked to the fact that national riders particularly shined in the moto-cross Grand Prix. Jacky Vimond became the first French world champion in 1986 on his 250 Yamaha, and Jean-Michel Bayle fell in behind him on his Hondas, in 125 in 1988, then in 250 the following year. The former would see his career shattered by a stupid "civilian" accident, but the latter would enjoy a superb career in the United States, before going back with some success to Grand Prix.

Jean-Michel Bayle, without doubt the greatest champion that French motorcycling has known in modern times, photographed in 1989 on his CR 250R.

The first French World Motocross Champion was Jacky Vimon. He dominated in 1986 at the controls of his Yamaha YZ 250, but would be grievously injured on the evening when he was to celebrating his victory.

The golden age of Paris-Dakar

After the death of Thierry Sabine in 1986, the "veterans" considered that Dakar had died with him. The event at least still retained exceptional public interest, which encouraged Honda to enter a very specific machine. This NXR would win the race four times in succession between 1986 and 1989, in the hands of Neveu, Orioli, and Lalay. A production version, the Africa Twin, would soon be charged with taking advantage of this success in business terms.

"The accident" Honda on trial

It is today difficult to understand what pushed Honda into investing in the marginal discipline of trials at the start of the 1980s : the lesson of the 1970s ought to have been enough. Whether it was the taste for a challenge, the envy to quickly make up for the unfortunate NR experiment ? At any rate, the Belgian Eddy Lejeune became world champion in the discipline three times in succession (from 1982 to 1984) with a four-stroke Honda.
Everybody considered this feat impossible, but Honda did it, and without gaining the slightest commercial benefit—they had few motorbikes for sale in this speciality—but merely for the beauty of the gesture. Since then, with total logic, the two-stroke reigns as master in trials and the "pom-pom" of the single cylinder is no more than a memory.

A number one for nothing

Exceptional performance of Bubba Shobert in the American championship : at the controls of his Hondas and notably the dirt-track RS 750D, he won the supreme title in the United States in 1985, 1986, and 1987. This was a particularly remarkable feat since Harley-Davidson had been winning this title without interruption since 1975, until Ricky Graham stopped this run in 1984 with his Hondas.
Very soon after this fine performance, the American Federation reorganized things so that Honda was eliminated from the competition by a rule modification. And to a man, the American customers would follow the order : Honda had sold more than 776,195 motorbikes in the United States in 1984, but would sell no more than 287,854 in 1988. Could it happen any other way ? So it is that, since then, calm reigns at the US championship : Harley-Davidson calmly dominates, nobody tries to mess competitively any more, especially Honda, cured by this distressing experience !

Externally, the Honda NXR looked like the commercial version of the Africa Twin, but this was a real works machine whose V-twin engine of 780 cc, with four valves per cylinder (three valves for the production engine) was rated at over 80 hp. Here is the NXR, making its debut in 1986 in the hands of Cyril Neveu.

Eddy Lejeune would be the only rider in history to use a four-stroke to win the scrambling World Championship, in this case with this RTL 360 of 1982.

The RS 750D basically had the same engine as the production XLV then Africa Twin, but it would fitted out with four valves per cylinder to produce 90 hp.

A return to the roots

Although there was an initial braking on Wall Street in 1987, the brutal crash of the Tokyo Stock Market
would not occur until 1990. In the meantime, Japan had been living inside its speculative bubble and had scarcely
suffered from the recession which had hit the West. After the focusing on the domestic market in the 1950s, after the
bipolarisation of the 1960s (Japan-USA), after the tripolarisation of the 1970s/1980s (Europe joining
the previous two large markets), the 1980s then 1990s would refocus on Asia to the detriment of America.

*The Taiwanese make Kymco started up under Honda leadership. It has since broken free, notably with this 125 Zing,
of which 10,000 examples have been sold in France from 1997 to the present day.*

his swing across was completely natural. The Asia of the 1980s was expanding fast, and the Big Four were carrying out profitable business there that would wipe out the relatively light troubles on the other markets. This strategy had been maturing over a long period. On the island of Taiwan, Honda had licensed production agreements since 1961. And when in 1988 this island was observed for the first time to have an output of over one million powered two-wheelers, this included three makes smelling fragrantly of Japan : Kwang Yang (Kymco) and San Yang (SYM) with Honda technology, YMT under Yahama control. Taiwan is today the world's fourth-largest manufacturer.

China over ten million

Japan is also present in continental China. When, after the death of Mao in 1976, China partially opened up to international co-operation, it had to restructure a great many weapons factories, qualified personnel, and efficient tools. Honda, like Suzuki, took advantage of this loophole beginning in 1978. It was not therefore astonishing that in 1993, the manufacture of powered two-wheelers in the People's Republic of China had ended up overtaking that in Japan. In 1997, Chinese output

If, in 1993, China has become the top world manufacturer of powered two-wheelers, it is thanks to Xing-Fu who manufacture Honda derivatives like this one.

even burst beyond the ten million mark, or almost four times more than Japan !

Today, Qingqi, largest world and Chinese manufacturer makes little Suzuki-based scooters, while Jialing, following hot on their heels, has direct contacts with Honda. Each of these Japanese makes have nurtured several alliances in this country, whose very extensive territory leaves considerable autonomy to each make across its immense regions.

In 1996, even India finished by relegating Japan to third place for world manufacturers of powered two-wheelers, again with makes under strong Japanese influence like Bajaj (Kawasaki), Escorts (Yamaha), Hero and Kinetic (Honda) or TVS (Suzuki).

It is in India that Kawasaki has the exclusive deal for licensed production. This 100 cc Champion 4S was one of the state-of-the-art models from Bajaj in 1994.

The Korean Daelim, initially linked with Honda, today has complete autonomy. Their 125 Daystar met with a real success on the French market in year 2000.

Korea, having for its part turned relatively quickly towards the automobile, its two-wheeler manufacturers had not had the time to swell to the same proportions as its neighboring countries. Daelim has, however, grown bigger since 1962 under Honda supervision, and Hyosung under that of Suzuki.

As for other countries in the region, they were equally very dependant on Japanese manufacturers : Honda has been present in Thailand since 1966, in the Philippines since 1973, in Indonesia since 1977, in Pakistan since 1983, in Vietnam since 1987. Only Malaysia has kept its distance, by more or less nationalizing its auto-moto industry under the protective wings of its powerful petroleum industry.

After the simple alert, a real crisis

In short, the crisis in 1990 went by almost unnoticed. Worse, Asia responded by thrusting its growth forwards even more, reaching a new summit in 1994-1995. But the roots of the problem had been not been treated. And a repeat of the upheaval that broke out in Thailand in July 1997 would contaminate the whole region. The situation was crystal clear; too expansionist, all these nations had lost the sense of proportion in orchestrating excessive growth, simultaneously by doubtful borrowing and dangerous loans. Their artificial "bubble" would end up bursting.

Some countries found themselves in a situation of virtual bankruptcy: in Indonesia, the automobile market was reduced to one seventh of its sales between 1997 and 1998 ! Everyone suffered, in different degrees, from excessive debt, including Japan, which had not survived the slow-down of its activity since the oil crises of the 1970s, and was constrained to enter into unfavorable alliances with the West.

In the tire sector, while Bridgestone had taken over American Firestone in 1988, Uncle Sam's revenge took shape in 1999 with the buy-out of Dunlop-Sumitomo by Goodyear. Even with the automobile, the big maneuvers were spectacular : Ford has controlled 33.4% of

The Honda Varadero, launched at the end of 1998, has quickly become the reference for lovers of touring, as well as re-launching a craze for big trail bikes.

One of the most mass-produced ostensibly retro machines today is the 250 Kawasaki Estrella, direct heir even as far as its engine measurements (66 x 73 mm) to the 250 Meguro-Kawasakis of thirty years ago.

Mazda since 1996, Renault acquired 36.8% of Nissan in March 1999, and Daimler-Chrysler bought up 34% of Mitsubishi at the beginning of 2000. Finally, while General Motors already owns 49% of Isuzu, the American group further increased its hold on Suzuki (by 9.9%) and Subaru (by 20%) in 1999. Only Toyota and Honda have escaped this contagion.

The situation has been calmed on the motorcycle front. The four Japanese manufacturers were in a dominant position, and even a weakened Japan was not enough to handicap them. Despite everything, a sign of the time, Toyota was increasing their participation in Yamaha at the start of the year 2000.

Export, as prestige

Although weakened, Japan remained powerful. The dollar bottomed out at 78 yen in April 1995. Systematically under-valued since the war by a Central Bank whose priority was export, the yen had begun to return to a normal rate with long-lasting pressure from "the American friend", and having admitted the necessity for a real exchange with business partners, it really picked up. The 1998 crisis would clean up this economy, but Asia would soar even higher in 1999. While the euro exchanged against 135 yen at its birth in January 1999, it would be worth clearly less than 100 yen eighteen months later.

This over-precious yen would step up the relocation of production, in particular for the lower-powered models whose manufacturing costs were crucial. For the first time in 1995, the Japanese industry (all sectors included) would invest more abroad than on national soil. Honda even ended up in 1996 by producing more automobiles outside Japan than at home. And above all, out of the 50,000 two-wheelers imported into Japan in 1998, over one third came from Taiwan. Certainly, this only concerned scooters, but in volume it was more than Harley-Davidson and more than all the European makes put together!

This new balance of power meant that the Japanese and above all the European markets were no more than showcases of prestige, which bought up the motorbike with big profit margins but in relatively limited numbers, while Asia sold small vehicles made on site, at feeble unit profits but in huge quantities.

Europe remained the primary export market for two-wheelers, with 700,000 machines per year, France and Germany in the lead with about 170,000 units each. This figure, two times superior to exports into North America or into Asia, took on a big tactical importance when the Japanese home market fell to around the million mark. The US market, which had become almost secondary, saw itself abandoned by the manufacturers: Honda which held 60% of this market in 1985, held no more than 30% by 1993 and scarcely seemed to suffer from it or to want to return to a better penetration.

Calming things down

With this new focus towards the East, the makes deployed a cautious policy in the West. Their lower-powered machines were threatened by "exotic" productions, Korean, Taiwanese and even Chinese, obliging them to place an even stronger accent on the "big cubes", where Aprilia, BMW, Ducati, Harley-Davidson and Triumph were their only direct competitors.

Although turnover figures for 1999 came back onto a par with those of thirty-five years before, the manufacturers had been more powerful in those days, primarily because "outside-Japan" production represented a growing part of the activity—then because the motorbike did not represent more than 40% of Yamaha's turnover, less than 15% for Suzuki and less than 10% for that of Honda.

The automobile continued to increase in carrying more weight, even with Yamaha, who were developing and building engines for Toyota, Ford, and even Mazda, or

For Japanese manufacturers, the lower-powered issue involves in coming up with new ideas, as Yamaha have been able to do with their large-tired TW generation. Appearing in 200 cc, this machine created a real fashion craze in Japan and its 125 version has been very well received in France. Here is a very Japanese-looking customized version.

Coming after the 400 of the same name, and before the 1200, the 600 Suzuki Bandit of 1994 followed an obvious formula : a sinewy motorbike, modern and fulfilling, but very simple and at a rock-bottom price. The market had not been misjudged and this roadster received a warm welcome, which made it into a European best seller and, in France the best of the above 125 cc from 1995 to 1998.

Rarely did a motorbike play the retro card with such coherence and rigor as the Kawasaki W 650. "W" for W1, of course, but with a British personality and a classical identity astoundingly close to the real thing. At a time when westerners were reviving makes like Triumph, Norton, Indian, Excelsior-Henderson, Bultaco, MV-Agusta, Benelli, Gilera or Mondial, why shouldn't Kawasaki take legitimate advantage of the Meguro line ?

Since 1999, Suzuki has cleverly renewed the idea of the roadster with its V-twin-engined SV 650s. The basic SV is a lightweight and lively machine, its S version is an economical racing version, freely influenced by the Ducati SS... but more civilized !

Honda's CB 900 RR Fireblade (here in its 1991 version) would certainly earmark the turning point of the 1990s in the hyper-sport sector.

with Kawasaki who were designing transmission systems for industrial vehicles.

It was only with this last manufacturer that the motorbike tended to progress (it climbed back to 20% of their turnover), following the decline in shipyards, steelworks, and civil engineering. As a rough guide, the motorbike had still represented 47% of Honda's turnover in 1975.

Nostalgia markets

The first application of the trend toward past glories came with the Kawasaki Estrella (1992), then with the remarkable Kawasaki W 650 of 1998. But it might well

A bad card : Kawasaki, in attempting to distance themselves from the Harley-Davidson school for its custom bikes, created a Drifter family influenced by the Indians of the 1940s.

The Yamaha XV 1600 Wild Star is the most powerful big twin of the time. Its belt drive and valve rocker mechanism make it a clone truer to nature than the Harley-Davidsons.

The 800 Suzuki Marauder of 1996 has innovated in the "customized" niche by its rather sporty look, resembling the dragsters.

have been that this phenomenon had been born with the… Yamaha SR of 1978, which is still in the catalogue twenty years later!

In this context, there nothing astonishing about the return of the pared down roadsters : what better than a super-sports model, uncomfortable at 56mph? Whether they were modern (like the Honda Hornet), sporting (like the Suzuki SV), classic (like the Suzuki Bandit), or ancient (like the Kawasaki ZRXs or Yamaha XJRs) or simply sensible (like the Yamaha Diversion), these "basic" machines were re-assuring and above all less expensive than the "supersports" ; even if it were only for the fact that in a tumble one did not crumple the bodywork.

In the same line of thought, it was not astonishing to see the "customized" models become more radical in the style of Harley-Davidsons, while deteriorating technically and putting on weight aesthetically, like the

With their FZS 600 Fazer of 1998, Yamaha had completely understood their clients needs : a roadster appearance, but a real streamlining, real comfort, and real performance to satisfy both sportsriders and regular riders at the same time.

This is an ignored trend, but the Japanese have been very fond of original and modern roadsters before Europeans. The Honda Hornet, which Europeans know in 600 cc, appeared as a 250 cc and has been enjoying great success in Japan since 1996.

Mechanically based on the 1500 Gold Wing, in 1996 Honda had developed the F6C Valkyrie, six-cylindered but also with a very respectable power output and handling.

The old dream of the auxiliary-engined bicycle surfaced again in 1993 with the Yamaha PAS. Considered as a simple bicycle throughout most of the country, this machine benefits from a prestigious status, but its price still limits its distribution.

For two years, the Suzuki 400 Burgman would remain the biggest scooter on the market. Appearing at the end of 1998, using a bike-frame very close to its 250 version and a 32 hp single to liven up its 384 lbs. Capable of cruising at 87 mph, the 400 Burgman held onto a real "scooter" philosophy, while the new Hondas and Yamahas were undergoing a more profound change.

Honda from the ST 1100 (1989) to the Deauville (1997)

One of the rare market niches still eluding the Japanese in the 1980s remained that of BMW and the great open roadsters. Honda attacked this in the autumn of 1989 with their ST1100 Pan-European with its completely new longitudinal V4 engine. This machine would adopt an ABS system and an anti-skid TCS (a first for a motorcycle) as of 1992, then a combined and linked braking system as of 1996. It has cared for its "GT" image by organizing a rally exclusively reserved for "ST 1100" owners every year since 1990. The Deauville, launched in the autumn of 1997, tried a route in line with the Pacific Coast of 1988. Borrowing its engineering from the NTV 650 Revere and manufactured in Spain, the Deauville became the weekend motorbike of the trendy citizen, with its integrated suitcases. Light and compact, it was not meant for the highways, but numerous professional messengers ended up adopting it. It was one of the missing links between the scooter and the heavy and bulky "GT"s.

The ST 1100 became established as the reference point for long-distance touring, both by its very personalized configuration and by its extremely advanced braking system.

Despite a slightly superficial finish, the Deauville ended up finding its public, that of less wealthy users, looking for an unpretentious, human-sized real road bike.

Yamaha XV 1600 Wild Star. Others, on the other hand, tried more courageous ways, like the Kawasaki Drifter or the Honda F6C.

As for the desire to reinvent the basic bike, this seemed equally logical. The Yamaha PAS then Honda Racoon and Suzuki Love, electrically-assisted, bicycles flourished and attempted to recreate the missing link between the pedated and the powered two-wheeler.

Two-stroke or four-stroke ?

In the 1990s, the debate remained open. At the 1995 Dakar, Honda entered a prototype EXP-2, whose single-cylinder two-stroke was injection-fuelled and whose compression ratio was permanently piloted electronically to keep on the limits of pinking and pre-ignition. The Pantheon scooter would put this principle into mass production as of 1998, in a simplified form, with fuel supply by carburetor.

Yamaha always exploring

Faithful to its habits, Yamaha persisted at the end of the 1980s in their exploration of new niches. Such tactics met with several dead ends. The TDR concept for a racing two-stroke trail bike, in the superbike style,

In 1988, the 250 TDR opened up the way towards a return to basics for scramble bikes, based on the super-motocyclist formula, by favouring road-holding at the expense of off-road. With its twin-cylinder two-stroke, delicate in operation and in a not very popular cubic capacity bracket for France, the TDR has not caught on, but the idea has a future.

would only meet with a brief success in 1988 in the 250 cc class. It would be readapted with great fortune by a very satisfactory TDR 125. The 1993 GTS, itself a great open tourer with an innovative chassis would be little loved, too expensive, too heavy for a racing model, not comfortable enough for a GT, and above all aesthetically too puzzling.

All this did not prevent Yamaha from succeeding in some of their experiments, beginning with the TDM 850 of 1991, powered by the same twin-cylinder as the

The 125 Pantheon scooter has demonstrated Honda's two-stroke mastery : consumption, backfiring, and fumes are kept at levels close to the four-stroke. Unfortunately, Honda has decided to withdraw from mass production of two-stroke engines as of 2002. To follow their example, numerous manufacturers have since felt obliged to go over en masse to the four-stroke, despite the potential and the long-term progress made with two-strokes.

Too shocking aesthetically with its triangular front, the unfortunate 1000 GTS did not have enough visible advantages to attract enough buyers.

Frankly neither trail, nor really long-distance, the 850 TDM was intended to offer the best of both breeds. This original machine enjoyed a fine success in France, where close to twenty thousand examples have been distributed since 1991.

Super Ténéré. It remains an unrivalled best-seller for its niche. Its more sporting sister, the TRX 850 of 1995, gained unanimous support by its performances, but its style and its unsuitability as a two-seater have put off a lot of people who otherwise might be attracted.

The old recipe of hi-tech performance

For over a century, the motorbike has always been judged on its performance. And even if public authorities regularly threw a wrench in the works, the escala-

The 850 TRX had been developed for the Japanese market that only had eyes for the beautiful Italian models. The other side of the coin, Europe criticized it for too closely resembling the Ducatis with its tubular frame. Efficient, this motorbike stands out, as does the 1996 TDM version, by its con-rod assembly inclined to 270°, which with by its cyclic irregularity recreates the same sensations as a V-twin—Ducati-style.

Along the same lines as the CB 1100 R of the 1980s and of the Ducati 916/996, the Honda VTR 1000 SP1 was relatively exclusive, even if only for its price, neighboring on $ 14,000.
Here is a version of this machine that has won the 2000 Le Mans 24 Hours and is participating in the World Superbike Championship.

tion of horsepower and of miles-an-hour has never missed out on making the regular customer dream.
This history met with a new acceleration at the end of 1998 with the Suzuki GSX 1300 R Hayabusa, then at the end of 1999 with the 1200 Kawasaki ZX 12-R. A point in common for these two machines : a power output equivalent or superior to 175 hp allowing them a top speed approaching a real 190 mph. But more than

just their pure performance, one remains confused by the ease in riding these motorbikes, and paradoxically by their safety. Watch for others to go further with this madness.

Naturalization

Still powerful, but fearful of maintaining a local rivalry that would shelter them from protectionist intentions

In a classical school, but with stylistic features that have since been copied en masse, the Yamaha YZF 1000 R1, appearing at the end of 1997, demonstrates that radical sports machines, by putting the emphasis on pure efficiency, remain perfectly modern. Its very recognizable profile, with its twin spaced-out headlights, has established its reputation. The 600 R6, appearing one year later, has built up just as flattering an image.

It is its excellent profiling that gives such performance to the Suzuki Hayabusa. But its aerodynamical shape has not gained unanimous support, despite astonishing long-distance abilities. The protection offered by its streamlining is certainly not famous, but its general comfort is astonishing.

With the ZX-12 R, Kawasaki has re-established an architecture dear to its heart, on the Grand Prix KR 500 then on the 900 Ninja: a spinal column framework. This is a cast aluminium piece which enables the machine's width to be kept down, and therefore its aerodynamic resistance.

by consumer countries, the Japanese manufacturers have stepped up their policy of naturalization during the 1990s, and not merely by increasing production capacity of their Western factories.

Honda supplies engines to Piaggio for its GT 250 and 250 X9 scooters but also for the Gilera 125 Coguar. For their part, Yamaha supplies its engines to the little French manufacturer Scorpa, specialized in trail biking and who will be responsible for distributing this almost hand-crafted motorbike to Japan.

As for Suzuki, they are distributing engines to Cagiva for their 1000 Raptor and Navigator, to Beta for their 125 and 200 Alp, and are also collaborating with Aprilia in a little factory for scooter engines in Saint-Marin. Nor should we forget that Motori Minarelli, now under Yamaha control, supply half a million engines each year to European manufacturers for scooters and mopeds of 50cc naturally, but also for heavier machines like the Benelli 125 and 250 Velvet, Italjet 125 Millenium, Malaguti 125 and 250 Madison as well as the Aprilia 250 Leonardo.

Finally we should add the equipment suppliers, who have themselves ended up by creating bridgeheads in Europe. Showa (suspensions) has installed a factory in Catalonia, Spain, while their rival Kayaba is working alongside the Italian Paioli, and Itsuba now manufactures its electrical equipment in Italy.

Once again, nature

With earthquakes, volcanic eruptions, tidal waves, typhoons, Japan is a country that more than others knows about the precariousness of things. The ephemeral is the daily experience and the ancient is venerated for its fragile reputation.

Local religions, Buddhism and Shintoism, indeed the Confucian philosophy that characterises the entire Extreme Orient, are the spiritual expression of this fatalism in the face of the elements, and of this innate respect for nature, for ancestors, and for everything known through time.

Dying, they say, enables one to better be reborn, and this idea of a "regenerative apocalypse", this persistence of break-up, has turned the Japanese into big consumers in the larger sense of the meaning: as everything is perishable, one does not repair, one throws away, one recycles, one buys up the new, and this is an excellent stimulus for the economy; anchored in the past, Japan is not backward-looking.

Since 1923, Japan had however forgotten how much nature, sometimes, could become hostile to it. On January 17th, 1995, something reminded them of this: the earthquake at Kobe caused five thousand deaths. They were not expecting a quake of this size in the region (geologically less exposed than that of Tokyo), and neither the architecture nor the rescue operations had anticipated this event.

Beyond the human toll, the port, its roads, and the overall transportation network had been profoundly disturbed, and a great many factories found themselves disorganised, above all in a country where "just-in-time" delivery had become the norm. Kawasaki and Dunlop had been particularly affected but, as she had done for centuries, Japan picked herself up, bruised, of course, but also in a certain way, stronger than before…

Conscious of the precariousness of their situation, the Japanese were in fact convinced that their only wealth resided in work capacity and in a certain built-in self-discipline.

Overpopulation and apathy seldom work out. A huge advantage for a country resides in this consensus, which leads everyone to row in the same direction for the common good and the superior interest of the whole of society. The harmony of group results in individual well-being.

Even if it means "unique thought", and its obligatory colleague political cant, this ultimately denies individualism, favoring a harmonious façade avoiding any exterior dissonance for the outside.

"The nail which is proud must be pushed in", says an old Japanese proverb, and western companies have come into line with this for several years.

This disciplinary aspect has often brought Japan close to Germany. To this, one should also add a great cultural and racial homogeneity: the country counts at the most 1% immigrants, essentially Koreans.

Everyone, on their respective level, is aware of working for a collectivity, and sincerely believes that it is this that will in turn bring in the benefits. More than patriotism, this is about a civic sense, of social conscience.

Above all, the group is priority, a belief in the consensus as favored by co-operation. However, this does not only have good sides, since it encourages conformity, inhibits initiative and individual development, and slows down decision making.

Support necessary for sales

Once the four Japanese manufacturers had become big industrialists, racing hardly ever again served to develop machines for mass production but instead to support simple sales promotion.

Of the three Aoki brothers, Haruchika is the one with the most flattering racing history.
He has twice been World Champion in 125 on Honda in 1995, as in this photo, and in 1996.

ith the lower-powered machines becoming immensely popular in the Far East, Honda once again took part in 125 Grand Prix racing in 1988. They would be followed by Yamaha in 1993.

The maneuvre, at the same time, enabled them to promote the Japanese riders. So it was that after the world title of Tetsuya Harada (250 Yamaha) in 1993, then that of Kazuto Sakata (125 Aprilia) in 1994, Haruchika Aoki in turn became World Champion in 1995 and 1996 at the controls of a Honda RS 125. Sakata would regain his crown in 1998. Besides, many Japanese riders would from now on take part in the world championships, and merely with a token role: in 125 of course, where Azuma, Manako, Ueda and Ui were regularly in the vanguard, in 250 with Nakano, Matsudo, Ukawa and Katoh, in 500 with Abe, Okada or Nobuatsu Aoki, in Superbike with Haga (Yamah), Yanagawa (Kawaski), and Fujiwara (Suzuki), in scrambles with Funinami (Honda).

If the supreme title in 500 had for the moment eluded Japanese riders, the factories busied themselves to help them finally win that crown: Honda, Yamaha, and Suzuki all made their "works" riders race in this prized class. Japan would besides have been the last country to abandon the 500 class for their own national championship. Since 1996, one quarter of the world championship Grand Prix took place in the Asia-Pacific region (two races in Japan, one in Malaysia, one in Australia), while waiting for China or Korea to join the club. In addition, one Chinese team contested all the events of the 2000 Enduro Championship. It is however, Malaysia that appears the most advanced in this field: a rider by name of Sharol Yuzy has regularly taken part in GP 250 during the 2000 season, the Hong Leong Group has entered the 500 MuZ in Grand Prix racing in 1998 and 1999, and the Modenas make, subsidiary of the automobile manufacturer Proton, hence of the big petroleum group Petronas, has since 1997 charged former champion Kenny Roberts with building up a racing stable in GP 500.

Fujinami confirms himself as the best Japanese trials biker. He is hot on the heels of his leader, Doug Lampkin, at the controls of this Montesa Honda in the 2000 Championship.

Californian Wayne Rainey, triple champion of the world in 500 for Yamaha, here during his second title campaign in 1991.

Texan Kevin Schwantz during his Grand Prix debuts in 1987, and his streamlined Suzuki.

"Go East". This command was obviously commercial, but it also corresponded as in Formula One, to ever stricter regulations in the West concerning publicity for tobacco and alcohol.

With Philip Morris and their Marlboro label remaining the principal backer of the world championships, it became necessary to organize the Grand Prix circuit in "tolerant" countries, where sponsors would not be obliged to cover up their logos. In addition, while tobacco consumption stagnated or diminished in the western countries, Asia remained an expanding market for the manufacturers, and they stepped up their promotional efforts in this region.

Even the arrival of four-stroke engines in Grand Prix racing, programmed for 2002, highlighted this commercial approach : what was the good of racing two-stroke machines that had nothing in common with the machines on sale to the customer ? "We agree to spend more, but for motorbikes that —more or less— might resemble production models." That is what made the superbike successful, where all the Japanese makes were permanently entered in an official capacity, which had never been anything other than very sporadic for Grand Prix. Accepting this, budgets would have to undergo a significant increase. But the ultimate role of racing would be accomplished : image promotion and sales.

Sport, however, is not exclusively based commercial considerations, even if the world speed championships had been organized since 1992 by a Spanish private enterprise. Human greatness would give it a chance of

Max Biaggi, by stringing together four world titles in 250 from 1994 to 1997 would make his mark on this medium-powered category. Three of this crowns were won on an Aprilia, but it was with this Honda that he clinched the final one.

Australian Michael Doohan won five consecutive titles in 500, something that had not been seen since the Agostini epoch.

The 500 Honda NSR in its 1992 version. In its rise to power, this machine even today touches 200 hp.

In 1999, Sébastien Tortelli remained with Jean-Michel Bayle the only French rider to have twice been World Moto-cross Champion. Here he is on his 250 Kawasaki in 1998.

flourishing, with success and above all with adversity. Three great champions would thus mark the 1990s in GP 500 : Californian Wayne Rainey, Texan Kevin Schwantz and the Australian Mike Doohan.

The first would win three titles in a row for Yamaha, in 1990, 1991 and 1992, before suffering a terrible accident at Misano in 1993, which would leave him paraplegic. The second would only win one title, in 1993, for Suzuki. But the level of his duels with Rainey, the energetic nature of his acrobatic riding, and consequently his many tumbles, as well as his great respect for the public would make him the spectators' favorite. Disappointed by the drop in intensity of the races after his rival's accident, saddened perhaps by not having gained his crown in Rainey's absence, he pulled out of racing soon afterwards.

And finally, the third would with Honda enjoy a fantastic career, such as had not happened since Agostini. His rise would however be brought to a halt in 1992 while he was leading the championship, after a fall in which he lost partial control of his right leg.

But Doohan would return stronger then ever and would devour five titles in a row in 1994, 1995, 1996, 1997 and 1998. A final fall in 1999 as he was about to gain his sixth crown, ended his career.

In all these disciplines, the Japanese makes more or less kept their supremacy. Punctually, various European manufacturers arrived to threaten them: Aprilia or Derbi in speed, Ducati or Aprilia in Superbike, Husqvarna or KMT in motocross, Beta in scrambling, Gas Gas or Husaberg in Enduro, Cagiva or BMW in long-distance rallying. But overall, motorcycle racing still bears the Nippon seal, which is absolutely logical given its world hegemony on the industrial front.

At least French drivers have their place in this panorama. The most glorious is without doubt Stéphane Peterhansel, six times winner of the Paris-Dakar, victorious in the 1992 Paris-Peking, world Enduro champion for Yamaha, and who has since enjoyed a brilliant career on four wheels.

But Sebastien Tortelli, twice world moto-cross cham-

As is customary, it is in the categories neglected by the other manufacturers that Kawasaki have been especially illustrious. Endurance, entrusted to a French organizing body have enabled them to harvest numerous laurels, notably with this machine in 1991.

pion for Kawasaki in 1996 (125) and 1998 (250), Frédéric Bolley, World Moto-cross Champion on a 250 Honda in 1999, and Stéphane Chambon, World Supersport Champion for 1999 also stand out. And one might have evoked the multiple titles of Vieira (1991), Morillas (1994), Mattioli (1995), Lavieille (1998) and Orgeix (1999), in a discipline which remains a French speciality, Endurance.

It was unfortunately when the "Dakar" had lost its audience that Stéphane Peterhansel and his Yamaha Super Ténéré began to dominate it head and shoulders. Inset: Peterhansel at the finish of a special Paris-Peking.

The prototype EXP-2 entered by Honda in the 1995 Dakar ought to have announced a new generation of more ecological two-strokes.

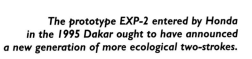

Will the future of long-distance rallying, and indeed of the motorbike in general, go over to two-wheel drive machines ? This is a hackneyed subject, revived some time ago by Yamaha, who won the Sardinia rally with this configuration in 1999. This is a hydraulic pump positioned above the exit gearwheel, transmitting about 10 % power to the front wheel.

Towards all-wheel traction

Where transmission is concerned, the most intriguing research field is without doubt that of the two-wheel drive. One recalls some efficient experiments by the Savard brothers at the end of the 1980s, then several trade show prototypes in 1991 that generated in the interest from the big factories for this new technology. One had also seen three Suzukis with shaft-chain drive and the Honda Mantis with its totally hydraulic transmission.

This is the path that is now being followed by Yamaha in collaboration with their subsidiary Öhlins with a very special TT 600, which has been seen in succession in 1999 finishing second in a rally in Sweden, then first in the Sardinia rally, before entering the Dubai rally with less success ; this promising technology ought to be with our everyday motorcycles in the years to come.

Another world becomes our own

With the globalization of trade, Japan has shown the way. Its economic and social structures
of the 1960s and 1970s have served as a model, twenty years later, for western companies before
this country had in turn to integrate Western work methods in the 1990s. Here are some of these concepts
that the West has had to take on board so as to get back in touch with Japan.

There is nothing left to differentiate today's Japanese assembly line from its European counterpart.

A **multi-speed economy, depending on the size of the enterprises.**

If one is living in Japan within the relative comfort of the big companies, the businesses in the secondary zone to whom they are subcontracting and who themselves are providing work for an incredibly complicated web of small workshops, would differ as much as in a Zola novel.

As for as employers are concerned, the education level in Japan is directly related to the financial rank of the employer rather than to the hierarchical or the usage level. With this planet-satellite system, the importance of the parent company is a guarantee of protection : loyalty to suppliers is strong, longevity in contracts is real, confidence given to subcontractors almost blind (the idea of "zero stock" implies "zero fault") and enables the huge businesses to attain a suppleness and a ability to react quickly, which one might have considered incompatible with their size.

Conversely, the subcontractors are directly dependant on the parent companies, not only in terms of costs, delays, and quality control, but also for immediate survival : or in one word, capitalization. With the result that, with no risk of a sudden strike handicapping productivity, it no longer becomes necessary to diversify the sources of supply. This facilitates communication between the requisitioner and the supplier. It also means that such suppliers are more or less deeply involved in the conception of the product, and that they deliver finished sub-assemblies more than spare parts. One should not, however, forget that such with a structure, there is an ever-present threat of employment insecurity with the lower level suppliers. They are the first to serve as a fuse in the case of a problem, and it is onto them that flexibility is transferred. As for the loyalty of the big concerns in times of crisis, this, as with us, has become an elastic notion.

"Poor citizens in a rich country"

For a long time, Japan has been summed up in this way. Even though the relative impoverishment of Westerners and the progressive wealth accumulation of the Japanese has made this aphorism less harsh, there is still a basis in truth : the Japanese today remain "traditionally poor" rather than "get rich quick", and 55 % of households still did not have an access to a main sewer at the start of the 1990s !

The household capital of the average Japanese remains modest : he is rarely owner of his residence because the square foot is so dear. His long-term debt is moderate since his belongings are on the whole consumer products. His savings, in return, essentially controlled by the firm or the state, are enormous.

They serve for his children's education, their marriage ceremony, for health and pensions, so many situations where the high price, directly taken on by the individual, is considered quite natural.

This explains why following England in the nineteenth century, or the United States from the 1920s to the 1960s, Japan has become the banker of the world since the 1970s.

The deep involvement of personnel in the business

According to paramilitary principles that make each employee into a good little soldier, the discipline and the loyalty of the Japanese towards his employer have until now been linked to the fact the business was giving back to him, through a reassuring working environment, pleasing social relationships ("automatic" promotion reducing rivalry between individuals in the same group) and a real employment stability.

Salary, in such a context, lost its importance and this enabled businesses to amass colossal nest eggs. So much so that many social structures, at least with the big businesses, were integrated into the enterprise: mutual insurance, loans, purchasing co-operatives, sporting bodies, accommodation, eating and even hospitalization remained assured "internally", and little money came out from the circle of the business and its satellites.

Since the 1950s and until the last few years, the rate of "desk near the window" (equivalent to our cubicles, but less belittling) was therefore impressive. But in starting to make redundancies in Japan, it was not long before several crises in confidence occurred. If "official"

For almost twenty years, Honda has bee producing articulated tricycles like this Stream, regarded with great affection by canteens and fast food distributors !

The covered scooter has been the city dweller's longstanding dream. Without going further than the BMW CI, Honda (here with the Cabina) and various accessory makers have sometimes built them.

In the Harley-Davidson spirit, the Japanese no longer just copy the custom bikes: the Yamaha XVZ 1300 Venture Star aligns itself with the aesthetic codes of the famous Electra Glide models.

The 250 Yamaha Majesty of 1995, along the same lines as the Honda Spazio, prefigures a generation of large scooters no longer limited to urban travelling.

unemployment was at its highest in 2000, at a rate close to 5%, it hardly took into account the millions of fake jobs or merely honorary jobs in businesses. Quite simply, instead of doling out state benefits into workless and marginalized people, Japan had preferred until now to maintain them in a more gratifying framework and to leave them with the illusion that they still belonged to the world of work.

This certainly corresponded to a greater welfare society than our own, also less state-controlled (since it is the company that accepts the financial responsibility) but the price was without doubt no higher and above all, the individuals were less belittled. This was however a concept which was finding it ever harder to stave off globalization.

Japan is also changing

Other principles were more penalizing. For example, with promotion taking place more often based on seniority than on merit —at least with the big businesses- risk— taking in the enterprise was hardly ever encouraged. It often paid better to flatter one's superior (by spending evenings with him in bars) than to obtain objective results or to propose original ideas. This seniority-based promotion, which reduced the mobility of the salaried from one company to another, at least presented one advantage for the companies: it avoided a rise in salaries that might tempt away the good elements of one's rivals !

But everything comes to an end and today's Japan has met up with a spectacular revolution. An employee is no longer there for life, the employer of his own boss may change, and redundancy, formerly unthinkable, has made its appearance in the big firms.

Twenty years ago, to remain loyal to their undertakings regarding their employees and to avoid being separated from them, a business hit by the recession was able to "lend" several thousand employees to other companies belonging to the same banking group. This is no longer the case today : there is no hesitation in making staff cuts. Equally, the tradition in Japan was to grant between fifteen and eighteen months' salary to employees, the bonus usually being paid out in June and in December. In addition, one part of the salary was extensively paid out in the guise of overtime or of free gifts.

With the recession of the 1990s the industrial world had been able, without any official reduction on the payslip, to correct the average revenue while paying out no more than twelve or fourteen months of salary, and in restricting the practice of bonuses.

Finally, we should not forget that, having got going in the 1950s, the present-day motorbike manufacturers have until now been free from their own burdens normal for standard businesses. Since then they must pay out more and more pensions to employees taking retirement, given that the average age —and salary— of their employees is increasing, they find themselves faced with problems until now non-existent.

Not everything is good to take up again

Certain elements of the Nippon success, linked to purely local factors of history or culture, were obviously not applicable in the West. Nor would others necessarily be advantageous to Japan. For example one of the great mysteries of Japan, for the Westerners, lies in its

Honda Shadow, Yamaha Dragster and Suzuki Intruder continue to seduce motorcycle buyers, by offering the look and sensations of a 125 cc "Harley-style" V-twin.

distribution system. Some automobile manufactures have been able to maintain up to five distinct networks, each one distributing a part of the range.

Marketing in Japan is in fact very delicate, particularly for young importers or manufacturers who must carve out a niche for themselves by penetrating existing networks and for a variety of reasons : Lack of space prevents the dealers from stocking over-extensive ranges with corresponding spare parts.

The saturated road network complicates transportation, and this is a particularly heavy handicap for "just-in-time" supply or for parts delivery.

Japanese consumption, although hungry for novelties and curious about the future, is largely based on loyalty and confidence. In short, new arrivals are rarely warmly welcomed, and this mistrust does not only occur where foreigners are concerned : even new Japanese makes must prove themselves before public acceptance.

Honda, not long ago, was again finding difficulties in building up a distribution network for their automobiles. Locally placed in second place behind Toyota and in front of Nissan, they are safe today, but they took a half century to establish themselves.

In the year 2000, it was the latest Honda 900 RR that took over from the Yamaha R1 and R6 for the title of the most distributed sports model on the French market.

Does the Suzuki DR-Z 400 herald a return of interest in ultra-light trail bikes, as much at ease in town as in off-road ? For the time being, it certainly remains desolate.

The Corin store in Tokyo is an eleven-story motorbike supermarket where one can find anything one might want in apparel and accessories for the practice of two-wheeling.

The Japanese customer is used to a quality level of service that costs business structures dearly. Packaging is more important in Japan than contents, and this applies both to presents and to purchases. The spectacle of the big stores is enlightening, with their bowing hostesses and their multiplicity of little paper bags for the slightest purchase.

The Japanese customer has to be seduced by canvassing at home, by incessant mailing, by personal and follow-up relationships with the salesman, by supplementary little services. To remain a customer, he must be loyally followed-up by after-sales service, for which there are a multiplicity of casual jobs, institutionalized for a long time in Japan.

Honda 900 RR, Yamaha R6, Suzuki GSX-R 750, or Kawsaki ZX-9R : the family of "supersport" machines remains extremely enduring. With ever diminishing weight and endlessly improved performance, these increasingly track-racing machines are less and less exploitable on open roads.

Some good lessons, all the same

George Orwell would doubtless have denounced this economic model, which puts up a feeble case for personal development for those whose center of interest is not the professional domain. But Western businesses have certainly been obliged to submit to this pattern for several years. And their only consolation is to realize that their autonomy has been at this price: if they had not adapted to Japanese formulae, they would have without doubt been purely and simply swept aside, or even colonized, which was hardly preferable.

This happened to a number of them, and did not save them from severe ordeals. Because in the opposite sense, from the West, Japan has learned employment insecurity and the loss of confidence in institutions. The average Japanese has lost his gullibility, at the same time he was gaining in independent thinking, as Japanese business has since then been encouraging (albeit still very moderately) creativity and personal initiative from which they have learned to benefit. In short, one is witnessing a readjustment of the structures of society, the globalization of trade finally leading to the standardization of ways of doing things. And suddenly therefore, Japanese society no longer has

the real advantage, since even the nest egg amassed during the "fat cow" period shattered with the financial bubble and the crash. That said, and concerning more precisely the motorbike, the Japanese manufacturers still have a good lead. Their former Chinese,

Taiwanese, Korean, or Indian licensees will undoubtedly gain in autonomy, but they are still a long way off from reaching total power. The Japanese motorbike, already rich in a long and dense history, still has some fine days ahead of it. A plus point to Yamaha for having

In Japan, space is at a premium, and the contrast between the sophistication of the machines and the way in which the dealers are working when they repair your motorbike is striking.

The Ueno quarter of Tokyo brings together all the motorbiking activities of the capital. The shops, as must be in Asia, spill out onto the narrow street.

A little halt opposite Lake Kawaguchi, the preferred tourist destination for Japanese bikers. The Japanese roads, essentially mountainous, easily lend themselves to motorbiking.

The astonishing Yamaha 500 T.Max develops 40 hp and touches 100 mph. Never have the harmonization of the scooter with the motorbike been brought so close together.

beaten Honda by a neck's length in presenting their "maxim-scooter" ahead of them. The T.Max500, unveiled in July 2000, resumed the concept that had been so successful with the Majesty (almost eighty million examples sold in Europe in five years) in marrying a sporting style with the practical realities of use : protection, baggage locker and comfort. Original, the engine is a parallel twin-cylinder positioned almost horizontally between the rider's legs. It is coupled to a variable-speed drive and rear-wheel transmission is effected by two chains in series under an enclosed cowling, in a motorbike swing arm.

APPENDICES

The four big makes, output, export, and home market.

Year	output Honda	export Honda	home market Honda	output Kawasaki	export Kawasaki	home market Kawasaki	output Suzuki	export Suzuki	home market Suzuki	output Yamaha	export Yamaha	home market Yamaha	
													1950
1950	531												1951
1951	2 380												1952
1952	9 699												1953
1953	29 797 (#1)												1954
1954	30 344			200						0			1955
1955	42 557						9 079			2 272			1956
1956	55 031(# 1)			5 083			18 444			8 743			1957
1957	77 509			6 793			29 132			15 811			1958
1958	117 375			7 018			66 363 (# 2)			27 184			1959
1959	285 218			10 104			95 862			63 657			1960
1960	649 243	36 978		9 261	139		155 445	2 841		138 153	4 734		1961
1961	935 859			22 038			186 392			129 079			1962
1962	1 009 787			31 718			173 121			117 908			1963
1963	1 224 695	312 871		34 954	362		271 438	29 494		167 370	35 368		1964
1964	1 353 594			33 040			373 871			221 655			1965
1965	1 465 762	597 294		48 745	13 933		341 367	98 800		244 058	125 335		1966
1966	1 422 949			67 959			448 128			389 756			1967
1967	1 276 226			79 194 (# 4)			402 438			406 579 (# 2)			1968
1968	1 349 896		606 889	78 124		31 206	365 330		294 598	423 039		283 162	1969
1969	1 534 882		647 748	102 406		23 909	398 784		268 324	519 710		275 265	1970
1970	1 795 828	1 096 712	696 019	149 480	124 704	23 390	407 538	193 426	211 098	574 100	315 863	260 422	1971
1971	1 927 186	1 037 918		208 904	190 940		491 064	302 130		750 510	469 525		1972
1972	1 873 893	1 237 423	604 315	218 058	198 187	13 560	594 922	403 838	202 528	853 317	597 737	256 660	1973
1973	1 835 527	1 228 789	609 807	250 099	241 230	15 849	641 779	382 720	258 805	1 012 810	639 408	306 038	1974
1974	2 132 902	1 468 477	620 496	354 615	328 617	19 299	839 741	595 810	200 273	1 164 886	847 562	262 607	1975
1975	1 782 448	1 224 844	554 133	274 022	244 811	19 168	686 666	501 290	201 298	1 030 541	719 725	340 982	1976
1976	1 928 576	1 230 797	702 527	284 478	263 760	18 369	831 941	632 233	201 627	1 169 175	795 341	371 516	1977
1977	2 378 867	1 558 256	833 088	335 112	307 373	19 950	1 031 753	768 003	240 093	1 824 152	1 282 521	528 204	1978
1978	2 639 588	1 548 180	958 294	326 317	301 881	16 707	1 144 488	772 430	322 083	1 887 311	1 126 915	680 485	1979
1979	1 767 257	984 134	844 911	270 191	247 864	33 132	934 938	621 762	385 581	1 503 491	875 246	668 591	1980
1980	2 578 321	1 495 290	1 011 931	475 996	428 641	39 412	1 350 963	827 609	487 429	2 029 244	1 177 500	331 254	1981
1981	2 928 357	1 762 222	1 204 563	464 933	417 417	39 491	1 529 342	820 132	705 792	2 489 950	1 362 353	1 112 032	1982
1982	2 996 614	1 494 203	1 504 045	301 684	266 466	34 774	1 397 718	665 064	714 031	2 367 162	1 144 894	1 032 477	1983
1983	2 399 876	1 217 824	1 153 952	244 595	238 577	37 557	906 806	481 870	530 260	1 256 102	684 052	696 540	1984
1984	1 676 820	836 980	942 506	276 320	228 730	40 955	931 981	439 938	491 130	1 141 186	616 792	567 598	1985
1985	1 991 729	1 244 759	944 901	251 320	206 304	43 301	820 399	413 219	412 095	1 472 899	677 200	695 953	1986
1986	1 477 110	851 724	833 059	197 287	177 159	34 256	657 161	245 614	387 188	1 065 085	488 971	927 894	1987
1987	1 194 620	588 477	702 243	175 042	131 301	44 900	360 277	223 777	191 400	900 669	395 686	538 163	1988
1988	1 355 756	503 059	911 103	193 687	148 426	46 347	467 003	203 607	256 609	929 172	409 761	539 816	1989
1989	1 248 503	390 439	832 967	196 780	146 861	48 729	482 206	220 671	274 188	866 873	345 414	502 929	1990
1990	1 227 636	391 716	825 887	250 003	193 675	55 529	502 722	256 333	269 809	826 534	342 020	467 708	1991
1991	1 346 371	517 881	793 744	277 077	208 478	64 435	543 720	283 494	265 250	861 448	400 949	456 070	1992
1992	1 486 885	668 953	754 376	253 009	182 304	65 207	618 554	391 536	233 252	838 087	425 844	402 615	1993
1993	1 426 356		666 541	228 684		53 501	612 194		162 095	755 920		372 117	1994
1994	1 268 626		628 334	208 102		46 986	525 096		159 831	723 101		358 460	1995
1995	1 291 873		644 480	215 163		39 710	546 021		165 633	699 984		363 029	1996
1996	1 172 541		646 450	207 036		34 032	505 989		195 182	698 810		344 252	1997
1997	1 125 311		625 418	221 741		29 328	552 148		182 730	776 480		350 762	1998
1998	1 002 595		527 010	240 953		27 417	558 881		178 208	833 368		330 345	1999
1999	846 366	379 875	429 840	247 225	218 815	29 107	432 848	334 509	108 374	723 384	479 939	269 638	
	output Honda	export Honda	home market Honda	output Kawasaki	export Kawasaki	home market Kawasaki	output Suzuki	export Suzuki	home market Suzuki	output Yamaha	export Yamaha	home market Yamaha	

In brackets : the rank obtained that year in terms of output volume.

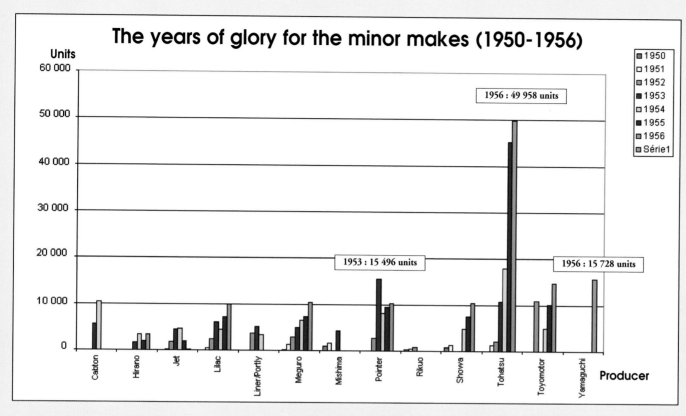

The years of glory for the minor makes (1950-1956)

Units

Legend: 1950, 1951, 1952, 1953, 1954, 1955, 1956, Série1

1956 : 49 958 units

1953 : 15 496 units

1956 : 15 728 units

Producers: Cabton, Hirano, Jet, Lilac, Liner/Portly, Meguro, Mishima, Pointer, Rikuo, Showa, Tohatsu, Toyomotor, Yamaguchi

Producer

The makes of average importance lived their golden age between 1950 and 1956. Notice among other things that Tohatsu had been Japanese market leader in 1955, ahead of Honda. The detailed figures per make are unfortunately unknown outside these years.

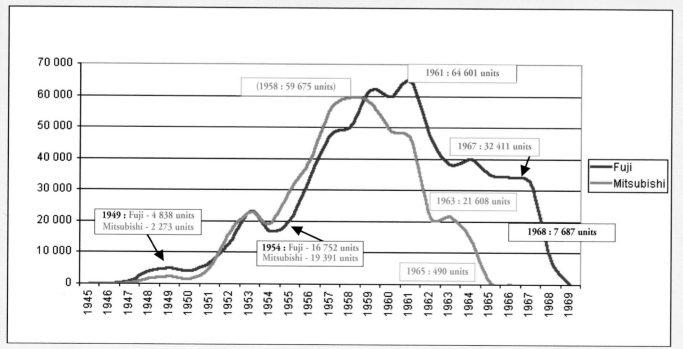

1961 : 64 601 units

(1958 : 59 675 units)

1967 : 32 411 units

1963 : 21 608 units

1949 : Fuji - 4 838 units
Mitsubishi - 2 273 units

1968 : 7 687 units

1954 : Fuji - 16 752 units
Mitsubishi - 19 391 units

1965 : 490 units

Legend: Fuji, Mitsubishi

While belatedly coming into line with the Italian school, Fuji managed to prolong a success from which Mitsubishi had to pull out, due to a heavy or sophisticated Japanese formula. In comparison, Piaggio Vespa output during the same period had already reached 10,535 units in 1947 and culminated in 330,914 in 1968.

The motorcycle in Japan from 1926 to 1961

Year	Total fleet (plus side-cars)	Home market	Total output	Total exports
1926	7 627+2 323			
1927	10 137+2 880			
1928	10 901+3 097			
1929	10 747+3 841			
1930	9 625+4 657		1 350	
1931	10 560+4 078		1 200	
1932	10 431+4 617		1 365	
1933	10 011+1 218		1 400	
1934	12 358+972		1 500	
1935	14 094+713		1 672	
1936	13 398+822		1 446	
1937	15 038+1 093		2 492	
1938	15 155+1 084		2 483	
1939	12 360+1 075		2 429	
1940	9 568+1064		3 037	
1941	5 062+811		2 596	
1942	4 370+702		2 189	
1943	3 450+593		1 965	
1944	1 603+484		1 029	
1945	2 304		146	
1946	2 869		470	0
1947	37 702°		2 858	210
1948	56 624°		9 692	1 112
1949	106 247°		7 371	547
1950	32 381**	46 870	9 803	845
1951	52 546**	83 008	24 153	491
1952	94 476**	176 506	79 245	18
1953	203 510**	349 308	166 429	105
1954	383 627**	504 770	164 473	191
1955	1 028 083	560 526	259 395	323
1956	1 266 553	667 654	332 760	648
1957	1 595 720	776 865	410 064	1 907
1958	1 965 669	897 306	501 332	5 427
1959	2 455 285	978 356	880 629	19 484
1960	3 038 474	1 425 688	1 473 084	56 268
1961	4 067 578	1 575 977	1 804 371	78 449
Year	Total fleet (plus side-cars)	Home market	Total output	Total exports

In 1979, Kawasaki contemplated replacing their three-cylinder 750 cc with this curious two-stroke prototype 750 cc with its two pairs of cylinders in tandem. It was never presented officially.

A fine future vision presented by the Suzuki Nuda in 1987. Its very aerodynamic lines, its twin-optic headlamp and its hydraulic integral transmission are today trendier than ever.

The first boom for the Japanese motorbike began in 1951, but it was not before the 1960s that really significant sales figures appeared.

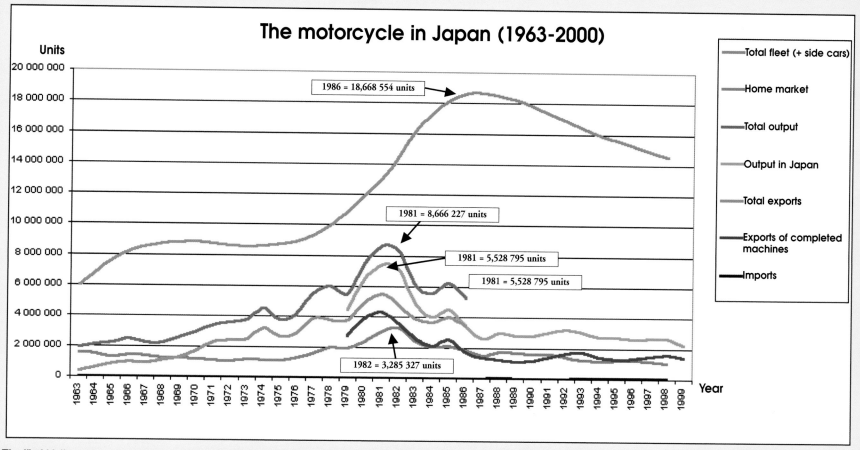

The motorcycle in Japan (1963-2000)

Units

Legend:
- Total fleet (+ side cars)
- Home market
- Total output
- Output in Japan
- Total exports
- Exports of completed machines
- Imports

1986 = 18,668 554 units

1981 = 8,666 227 units

1981 = 5,528 795 units

1981 = 5,528 795 units

1982 = 3,285 327 units

Year

The "bubble" expansion which started in 1980 will cost dearly from 1982 on, especially for the two majors, Honda and Yamaha.

Both exhibited at the 1999 Tokyo Motor Show, these prototypes announce (perhaps) tomorrow's motorbike : the Yamaha MT01 is a vision of roadsters to come, and the Honda X-Wing a glimpse of future open touring bikes.

Selective list of recorded makes in Japan

The other makes under which the products of the same company have been distributed and, where appropriate, the industrial group to which the make belongs, are indicated in the second column. The sign > indicates a takeover by another company or a change for trade reasons. These dates are approximate, the industrial start end do not always correspond with beginning or end of commercial activity.

Make	Company and other makes	Start	Finish	Town
Abe Star	Abe kugyustha	1930	1959	Tokyo
Aero Fast	NMC (Nippon Motors) engineer Shimazu	1925	1927	Osaka
Aichi Kikai	Giant			
Aikoku	JAC (Japan Automobile Company) > Nippon			
	Nainenki > Tokyu Kurogane	1933	1938	Tokyo
Aisan Pit		1953	1954	
Aiwa Motor				
Akebono		1953		
Angel		1953		
Arai	Arai Jidosha	1953	1955	Tokyo
Asahi	Miyata Works Limited (& Myapet)	1912	1964	Tokyo
Auto Bit		1952	1962	
Aviation		1953		
Baby Tiger	Iwasho Co.	1950s		Nagoya
BIM		1956	1961	
Bis motor		1946		
Black Horse		1954		
Blue Bird		1954		
BM		1954		
Bridgestone	Bridgestone Fuji Precison Co.	1952	1970	Tokyo
Cabton	Mizuho Jidosha	1932	1958	Tanba-gun
Center		1950	1955	
Central		1954		
Champion	Bridgestone Cycle Industry Ltd.	1960	1967	Tokyo
Chiyoda		1954		
Chubu		1989		
Crane		1955	1958	
Daihatsu	Daihatsu Kogyo Kabushiki Kaisha	1930	1979	Osaka
Darling		1956	1958	
Derby		1952		
Devil		1954		
DNB		1955	1961	
DSK	Daito Seiki Company Motorcycle Industries Co Ltd	1954	1960	Tokyo
Echo	Tosho Motors Ltd (cf. Pandra)	1958	1963	Tokyo
Emuro	Health Motor Industrial Co.	1945	1961	Tokyo
Flybird		1951	1956	
FMC Gasuden	Fuji Motors Corp. (Kreidler)	1951	1964	Tokyo
Fuji	Fuji Heavy Industries (Rabbit)	1946	1968	Tokyo
Fuji-company		1950 ±	1973	
Hayate		1955	1959	
Health	Health Motor Industrial Co.	1945	1961	Tokyo
Hino		1910		
Hirano	Hirano Seisakusho (Popet - Popmanlee - Valmobile)	1952	1961+	Nagoya
HKS		1973	1983±	Fujinomiya
HMC	Hyogo Motors	1931		Kobe
Hodaka	(Steen)	1964	1978	Nagoya
Honda	Honda Motor Co.	1946	---->	Tokyo
Hope Star		1952	1954	
Hosk	Yamarin (Yamada Rin seinkan Co)	1953	1960	Tokyo
Hurricane	Fuji Heavy Industries	1953	1958	Tokyo
Ideal Real Car	Yokoyama	1931		Kobe
IMC	Itoh Motor Corp. (Hayafusa)	1947	1961	Nagoya
International		1952	1957	
JAC	(Japan Automobile Company) Kurogane, New Era, Aikoku	1928	1934	Tokyo
Jet-Star		1953		
Jimmie		1950		
Jupiter Bike Star		1954		
Kanto		1957	1960	
Katakura Auto	Katakura Cycle co.	1958	1968	Tokyo
Kawasaki	Kawasaki Heavy Industries	1961	---->	Kobe
Kawasaki Aircraft		1953	1960	Kobe
Kawasaki Meguro		1959	1961	Kobe
Kawasaki Meihatsu		1955	1957	Kobe
Kitty		1954		
Komine	Komine (Giant, Wasp)	1924	1956	
Kongo	Fuji Kikai	1955		Tokyo
Kume Sankei	Kume Sankei	1956		
Kurogane	Nippon Jidosha >Kurogane	1937	1959	Hiroshima
Kyokuto		1950's		
Life	Nagamoto Hatsudoki	1953		
Lilac	Marusho Motorcycle Industrial co.	1948	1967	Hamamatsu
Liner	Kitagawa Motors Ltd	1952	1958	Hamamatsu
Linnet		1953		
Lion	Osaka bicycle	1926	1933	Osaka
Lucky	Yamato / Lucky	1953	1958	
Martin		1956	1961	
Maruichi	Maruichi Bicycle Company	1948	1959	Yokohama
Marushin		1954		
Maruto		1953	1954	
MBC		1953		
Meguro	Meguro Manufacturing Co.	1924	1961	Tokyo
Meihatsu	Kawasaki	1953	1961	Akashi
Midori		1952	1953	
Million	Itagaki Co.	1954	1961	Isesaki
Misima	Misima Kei Hatsukogyo	1950	1956	Misima
Mitsubishi	Mitsubishi Heavy Industries. (Silver Pigeon)	1946	1965	Tokyo
Miyata	Miyata Works Limited (Asahi & Myapet)	1912	1964	Tokyo
Monarch	Monarch (Pony)	1952	1962	Tokyo
Moon Tiger	Moon Tiger	1954		Osaka
New Day		1955		
New Era	Nippon Jidosha	1928	1937	Tokyo
Nikko		1959		
Nissan Bike		1950	1956	
NKB		1952	1956	
NMC	NMC Nippon Motors (engineer Shimazu)> Aero Fast	1912	1962	Osaka
Noritsu	Okamoto bicycle	1953	1954	Nagoya
NS Shimazu		1908	1909	Osaka
Ohyashima		1953		
Olympus	Katayama Sangyo (King)	1952	1962	
Pandra	Tosho Motors Ltd (cf. Echo)	1958	1963	Tokyo
Pearl		1952	1958	
Pet (Popet)	Pet (Popet)	1953		
Petty		1952		
Planet		1959		
Pointer	Shin Meiwa Industry Co. Ltd. (Ace, Pointer)	1949	1963	Naruo (Tokyo)
Praber		1952	1953	
Punky		1953		
Queen Rocket	Rocket Co. Ltd.	1950	1960	Hamamatsu
Rikuo	Rikuo Airstone	1935	1962	Tokyo
Ritsurin		1936	1953	
Road King	Fuji Kikai Co	1959		Tokyo
Rocky		1952		
Royal-Queen	Itagaki Co.	1954	1961	Isesaki
RSY		1954		Osaka
Rush (J)		1953		
Sankyo	Sankyo Electric	1950s		
Sanyo (Rotary)		1953	1962	
Shimpo		1952	1954	
Showa	Showa Works Ltd. (Cruiser)	1939	1960	Numazu
Silk (J)		1952	1960	
Silver Star		1953	1958	
Spark		1953	1955	
SSD	Shishido brothers	1930	1935	Hiroshima
Sumita	Sumita hatsudoki	1950	1955	Tokyo
Sunlight	Itagaki Co.	1954	1961	Isesaki
Suzuki	Suzuki Motor Corp. (SJK - Colleda)	1953	---->	Hamamatsu
Suzuran		1954	1956	
Sylbon		1951	1953	
Taf		1962		
Taiyo		1953		
TAS	Tanaka Kogyo	1955	1960	Chiba
Thomas (J)		1957	1957	
Thunder	Watanabe Takeshi	1925	1938	Osaka
Tohatsu	Tokyo Hatsudoki co. Ltd.	1948	1966	Tokyo
Tokei		1953		
Top Motor		1955		
Toyo Kogyo (Mazda)		1920	1960	Hiroshima
Toyo Motor (TMC)		1947	1961	Kariya
Tsubasa	Tsubasa Industry Co. Ltd.	1931	1960	Osaka
Tsuruwa		1952		
Giant (Wasp)	Komine	1924	1954	
Yamaguchi	Yamaguchi Bicycle MFG; Co. Ltd. (Marukui) (Hodaka)	1941	1964	Tokyo
Yamaha	Yamaha Motor Co. Ltd.	1954	----->	Iwata
Yamarin	Yamarin (Yamada Rin seinkan Co) (cf Hosk)	1951	1960	Tokyo
Yamato	Yamato / Lucky	1927	1958	
Young Man		1954		
YSK				
Z		1953		
Zebra		1961	1961	